FASHION & INTERIORS
A GENDERED AFFAIR

HANNIBAL

FASHION & INTERIORS

A GENDERED AFFAIR

Amber Valletta wearing a suit, photographed by Craig McDean for *Interview Magazine*, July 2014.

FOREWORD
        Kaat Debo —————————————————————— 6

INTRODUCTION
        Romy Cockx —————————————————————— 10

DRAPERY IN CLOTHING AND INTERIOR DESIGN 1865-1890:
EMBELLISHMENT AS A FETISH, STATUS SYMBOL AND DEFENCE
        Wim Mertens —————————————————————— 14

A WOMAN'S MOST VERSATILE FASHION ACCESSORY:
THE REUSE OF KASHMIR SHAWLS IN LATE-NINETEENTH-CENTURY
CLOTHING AND INTERIOR DECORATION
        Dries Debackere —————————————————————— 32

WEARING THE HOME IN TIMES OF TROUBLE
        Romy Cockx —————————————————————— 40

HENRY VAN DE VELDE'S METAMORPHOSIS: VILLA BLOEMENWERF
AND THE ROLE OF HENRY'S MUSE MARIA SÈTHE
        Werner Adriaenssens —————————————————————— 62

THE 'ELEVATION OF WOMEN'S DRESS' AROUND 1900:
WOMEN AND THEIR CLOTHES BETWEEN DECORATION AND
EMANCIPATION
        Magdalena Holzhey —————————————————————— 74

LINKING FASHION WITH ARCHITECTURE AND INTERIOR DESIGN:
THE WIENER WERKSTÄTTE, SCHWESTERN FLÖGE AND PAUL POIRET
        Lara Steinhäußer —————————————————————— 82

AT HOME WITH THE DESIGNERS: PAUL POIRET AND JEANNE LANVIN
        Jess Berry —————————————————————— 112

INTERWEAVING FASHION AND THE INTERIOR: THE MATERIALITY OF
LILLY REICH'S MODERN DESIGN
        Robin Schuldenfrei —————————————————————— 150

THE PHANTOM JACKET: LE CORBUSIER AND THE OBSCURE
LEGACY OF THE FORESTIÈRE
        Ian Erickson —————————————————————— 172

ANN DEMEULEMEESTER, MARTIN MARGIELA, RAF SIMONS
AND THE CROSS-POLLINATION OF FASHION AND INTERIORS
        Romy Cockx —————————————————————— 184

FOREWORD

Kaat Debo

In the spring of 2025, MoMu – Fashion Museum Antwerp – is presenting *Fashion & Interiors. A Gendered Affair* MoMu might be described as a lens through which to observe the world from different angles, exploring the limits of what fashion can mean and looking beyond the canonised stories from fashion history. The *Fashion & Interiors* exhibition reflects that mission.

In this book we bring to life the historical and present-day interconnection and complex relationship between fashion and interior, with a special focus on gender mechanisms. This exploration starts in the second half of the nineteenth century, a time when both fashion and interiors played a crucial role in affirming social status and gender roles. The (bourgeois) lady of the house was pivotal in conveying a carefully constructed image of elegance and sophistication, not only through her dress, but also in the way she furnished her home. The interplay of textiles, form and space tells a story of emancipation but also of restrictions within the gender roles of the time. During this period, the aesthetics of clothing and home décor merged into a shared visual language. Drapes, rich fabrics and ornaments were not only decorative elements but also symbols of power, status and femininity. Curator Romy Cockx and the authors of this book consider how these principles were applied, adapted and even challenged by designers and users, both men and women, and how fashion and interior continue to evolve and respond to changing ideas about gender, identity and space. A special place is set aside in the exhibition for three Belgian fashion designers – Ann Demeulemeester, Martin Margiela and Raf Simons – whose visual language and design methodology are a surprising echo of and reflection on the historical relationship between fashion, architecture and interior.

The exhibition would not have been possible without the support and collaboration of a number of researchers, designers, museums and lenders. Jelle Jespers designed the book and the campaign. Francesca Bonne and Veerle Van de Walle of Altu architecture studio designed the exhibition space and Victor Robyn the gallery texts. My special thanks go to curator Romy Cockx for putting together the content of this project and also to the dedicated MoMu team, who brought this ambitious exhibition to fruition. Also a special word of thanks for our partners, Vitra and the Vitra Partner Store Antwerp, as well as for Tanguy Van Quickenborne from the company Van Den Weghe.

Patty Carroll, Mad Mauve, *Anonymous Women* series, 2018.

INTRODUCTION

Romy Cockx

Fashion & Interiors. A Gendered Affair explores the relationship between fashion and the interior through the lens of gender. It begins in the second half of the nineteenth century, a period in which these two aesthetic forms were brought into play to consolidate the power and social position of the new (Western) bourgeois elite. The lady of the house played an important role in this: it fell to her to visualise the recently acquired status through her dress and tastefully furnished home.

The ideal of bourgeois domesticity divided the sexes into two separate spheres. While the husband went out to work, his wife would concentrate on injecting life into the home. With an eye on comfort, she would decorate it with soft cushions, curtains, handiwork and all manner of knickknacks. Her body too was heavily draped with layers of fabric and passementerie, causing her to seemingly merge with her interior.

At the end of the nineteenth century, male designers like Henry van de Velde and Josef Hoffmann waged war on that decorative excess and on women's fashion in particular. They can take the credit for two of Belgium's internationally renowned total works of art, Villa Bloemenwerf and Palais Stoclet, where they matched the interior and the lady of the house's garments, still emphasising her decorative role. Both the Van de Veldes' residence and Hoffmann's Wiener Werkstätte approach, however, show that women also made an active contribution to the Gesamtkunstwerk in spite of the limitations imposed by gendered norms.

Women also played an ambiguous role in the approach taken by the French fashion designer Paul Poiret. Although he found the Gesamtkunstwerk concept too extreme, his contacts with the Wiener Werkstätte inspired him to set up the Atelier Martine interior-design business, attached to which was a school where girls from working-class backgrounds created textile designs. Denise Poret played a pivotal role as the primary model in her spouse's lifestyle branding. Then there was Jeanne Lanvin, the first female fashion designer to reinforce her brand identity through interior design, a strategy that is followed to this day.

The total approach also attracted the attention of architect and cultural critic Adolf Loos. He derided Van de Velde and the effeminate Wiener Werkstätte, and demonised women's fashion. A pioneer of modernism, he favoured sobriety and functional male clothing, preferably bespoke British tailoring. He was followed in this by Le Corbusier, who not only commissioned a mysterious jacket for himself but in 1952 also designed garments for women. Moreover, both men's discourses display gendered parallels between fashion and (interior) architecture.

Despite the problematisation of bourgeois 'feminine' taste, some women designers still managed to forge a career in 'masculine' modernism. Lilly Reich is an interesting example: besides clothes, she also designed interiors, furniture and exhibition sets. Her collaboration with Ludwig Mies van der Rohe, however, also highlights the complexity of authorship and the male shadow of history.

The ways in which fashion designers have incorporated the interior into their visual language in recent decades mirrors the retrospective reassessment described above and the fragility of our Western approach to domestic comfort.

'Her sphere is within the household, which she should "beautify", and of which she should be the "chief ornament".'

(Thorstein Veblen, *The Theory of the Leisure Class*, 1899, 82)

Alfred Stevens, *The Visit*, c. 1870, oil on panel, Clark Art Institute, Williamstown, 1955.861.

1 Afternoon dress in shot silk fabric with floral pattern, silk velvet ribbon and silk fringing, c. 1855, MoMu, Antwerp, T21/1.

2 Désiré Guilmard, design for a window dressing, colour lithograph, from *Le Garde-meuble ancien et moderne*, 1839, album 60, plate 169, Cooper Hewitt, Smithsonian Design Library, New York.

DRAPERY IN CLOTHING AND INTERIOR DESIGN 1865-1890: EMBELLISHMENT AS A FETISH, STATUS SYMBOL AND DEFENCE

Wim Mertens

In an article about textiles at the time of France's Second Empire (1852-1870), draperies were labelled the fetish embellishment of both ladies' clothing and the domestic interior.[1] Looking at paintings, prints, photographs and other iconographical material from that period, leafing through fashion magazines and consulting upholsterers' handbooks, we can only conclude that the suggestion of fetishism with regard to drapery was justified. Drapery was idolised like a fetish. The veritable 'drape mania', however, only really took hold in the West in the last three decades of the nineteenth century.

SOCIAL CONTEXT: THE ENTRENCHMENT OF MIDDLE-CLASS VALUES AND NORMS

In terms of social organization, much was changing in Europe at that time, and not least in France, which was still seen as the paragon of fashion and *savoir vivre* in the West. After a period that saw the reinstatement of the French monarchy (1815-1848) followed by a short-lived phase as a republic (1848-1852), in 1852 imperialism was restored. That year Napoleon III Bonaparte, nephew of Napoleon I, ascended the throne, and during his rule, France became a prosperous nation. Technological advances and the monarch's favourable attitude to free trade boosted the movement of goods and existing and new industries and services, such as textiles, mining, chemicals and transportation. As well as a rich, even super-rich, class of entrepreneurs, this created a wealthy middle class. The social order was moulded to its values and norms. Money and upward social mobility, as opposed to a person's name and family tree, were now the measure of social success.[2] The bourgeoisie, rather than the nobility, were the real protagonists.

Paradoxically enough, the new middle-class elite in the West mirrored its lifestyle on the old European aristocracy. Though the latter's social role had been in decline for some time, it still spoke to the imagination of many. This applied both to the way they furnished their new homes and to their wardrobe. The constant interplay between bourgeoisie and aristocracy, between the past and the present, was characteristic of the time.

Interior design drew on the artistic idioms of the *ancien régime*: renaissance, baroque, rococo and neoclassicism. They were linked to the names of former French kings. A room was furnished in a particular historical style according to the purpose it served. The reign of Louis XV (1715-1774), which largely corresponded to the rococo, was considered the apotheosis of French culture.[3] Like the Louis XVI style, it was popular for salons and bedrooms.[4] So the rise and consolidation of that new civil society was played out under an emperorship, in a setting that referenced the *ancien régime*.

THE RENAISSANCE OF DRAPERY DURING THE SECOND EMPIRE

The influence of old-style idioms was also apparent in fashion, where Empress Eugénie and her entourage were for now setting the tone. Opulent courtly life with its resplendent balls was the great catalyst.[5] The empress' fascination with the French queen Marie-Antoinette (1755-1793) was externalised not only in the colours and patterns of fabrics, but also in their embellishments and cut.[6] The shape that characterised the eighteenth century, however, was interpreted rather than slavishly copied.[7]

Trailblazers for the new fashion trends were the Parisian *magasins de nouveautés* – or novelty stores – which stocked the latest fabrics and regularly also availed themselves of the services of seamstresses under concession agreements. These *magasins* often had direct links with the manufacturers,

3 André Adolphe Eugène Disdéri, portrait photograph of Lady Beresford, 1867, The Metropolitan Museum of Art, New York, Gilman Collection, gifted by the Howard Gilman Foundation, 2005.100.588.2.53.

4   Charles-Germain de Saint-Aubin, lady in court dress, watercolour, 1785, Musée des Arts Décoratifs, Paris.
5   André Adolphe Eugène Disdéri, portrait photograph of Guillemette-Josephine Brunold, Countess von Tieffenbach, 1862, J. Paul Getty Museum, Los Angeles.
6   André Adolphe Eugène Disdéri, portrait photograph of actress Berthe Girardin, 1866, Musée d'Orsay, Paris, PHO 1995 26 117.

4

5

6

7 Afternoon dress in rep silk, machine lace, silk satin ribbon and glass beads, c. 1870, MoMu, Antwerp, T12/395ABDC/J259.

8 Désiré Guilmard, design for a salon, colour lithograph, from *Le Garde-meuble ancien et moderne*, 1859, album 120, plate 348, Stiftung Fürst-Pückler-Museum Park und Schloss Branitz, Cottbus.

9 Gustave Léonard de Jonghe, *Mother with her Young Daughter*, oil on panel, 1865, private collection.

including the silk manufacturers in Lyon, the textile printers in Alsace and the muslin-weaving mills in Picardy.[8] Among them was *A la Providence*, a prestigious *magasin de nouveautés*, where between 1843 and 1858 Charles Frederick Worth was first a sales assistant and later a partner. In 1858, Worth went on to found his own fashion business in partnership with Otto Gustav Bobergh.[9] Worth's first creations followed the prevailing fashion for wide, round crinoline skirts. It was not long before he was attracting clients from Europe's highest echelons, including the French empress.[10]

At the beginning of the empire, embellishments on dresses were still discreet: strips of braid, ribbon, fringes or other passementerie were applied mainly to the bodice of the gown (Fig. 1). The same embellishments adorned textiles used to decorate rooms, such as chimney and window dressings. Simplicity and symmetry prevailed (Fig. 2).[11] The end of the 1850s saw an increase in embellishments on gowns. Pleated trims and flounced ruches, clearly inspired by eighteenth-century examples, came into vogue (Fig. 5), along with wide bands featuring large geometric designs such as meanders, diamonds and circles.

Around 1864, Worth introduced a new trend. He did away with the round, voluminous crinoline skirts, flattening them down at the front and moving the volume of the skirt to the back,[12] in part paving the way for a silhouette in which greater prominence was given to drapery. The drape effects were created in overskirts (Fig. 3), where they were held in place with passementerie, ribbons and (artificial) flowers. The overall effect was reminiscent of the lavishly embellished court gowns of the 1780s (Fig. 4).

Of a different order, but with a similar visual effect, was the drapery in the new, emerging fashion for walking dresses. Here the skirt was raised by means of metal eyelets on the inside of the skirt, which were attached to hooks on the underskirt or the skirt itself (Figs. 6 & 7).[13] This functional drapery was reminiscent of the old practice of lifting costly skirts to keep them clean outdoors.[14] The decorative effect of that pragmatic solution underlies the fashionable eighteenth-century *robe à la polonaise*, which became the inspiration for ladies' fashion in the latter years of the Second Empire.

Another cornerstone of fashion during the Second Empire is often described as *style tapissier*. Indeed, the dresses lavishly embellished with passementerie and ruches shared a clear correlation with the soft furnishings used in the domestic setting, where the upholsterer had an increasingly important role to play. Characteristic, too, were the fully upholstered seats, finished at the bottom with ruches and fringes, which had first come into vogue in the 1840s (Fig. 8). Empress Eugénie's passion for fabrics in interior design, her *goût tapissier*, did not go unnoticed among her contemporaries and was even derided in a vaudeville in 1851.[15] This imperial interest in home décor was considered bourgeois.[16] And indeed, in their private life, too, the imperial couple adopted bourgeois values. For example, special attention was paid to family, the new nucleus of civil society.[17]

CONSUMERISM IN TURBULENT TIMES

The Franco-Prussian War led to the deposition of Napoleon III in 1870 and the establishment of the Third Republic. It was a turbulent period during which supporters of the emperor fled the country, among them a number of couturiers.[18] A financial crisis followed in 1873, causing world-wide stagnation that lasted for decades. Despite the political and economic turmoil, some social evolutions and phenomena managed to stand firm and even make headway, one of them being the externalisation of financial and consequently social success by consuming and displaying all manner of commodities. This became an obsession and a status symbol in a now bourgeois society.

By this time, the former *magasins de nouveautés* were large department stores: shopping palaces stocking a wide range of fabrics for dressmaking and soft furnishing, *confections*[19] and accessories, beauty products, household effects and furniture. So the merchandise focused on fashion and interior, two spheres that for half a century and as part of the bourgeois narrative had increasingly come to be seen as the preserve of women.[20] Within that narrative, the distinction between what belonged to the male sphere and what to the female sphere was inherent. Moreover, it was every wife's moral duty to create a comfortable home as a breeding place for future generations, a safe haven in a hostile world. Both her clothes and her home décor were an expression of her inner self. At the time, that axiom applied to all social strata and was copied throughout the Western world.[21] An unkempt appearance of either the person or the home betokened reprehensible morals. The paintings of Gustave Léonard de Jonghe (1829-1893) featuring ladies in fashionable house dress in a comfortable interior seated over their handiwork while looking on contentedly at their daughters at play were less innocent than they might appear (Fig. 9). They show the aspirational ideal of the bourgeois woman.

In that context, fashion magazines became more and more popular. They were a source of *savoir vivre* for ever-larger groups of women. *La Mode illustrée*, the first fashion magazine with a large print run and targeted at upper-middle-class ladies, provided not only information about the latest fashion trends and designs for all manner of handiwork, but also housekeeping tips. From 1860 their pages also featured the occasional section on interiors with recommendations its female readers could follow according to their budget. The choice of textile played an important part in this.[22] Other journals followed, including outside Europe.[23] In addition, fashion magazines published sewing patterns as supplements. Initially they were simple, small-scale line drawings comprising few, if any, instructions. Their use did require a good grounding,[24] but then learning to sew and execute handiwork was a set part of a girl's education at the time. Readers could either engage the services of a professional seamstress or set to work on the patterns themselves. Sewing machines, which were becoming increasingly common in private homes, not only reduced the time it took to make a garment but also speeded up the application of embellishments.

The combination of the rise in popularity of the sewing machine, greater access to new trends in fashion and home décor provided by the fashion journals, the ever-expanding range of fabrics of different qualities and prices in the department stores, and not least the revival of historical styles all contributed to the drapery mania that took fashion and interior design by storm.

THE HEIGHT OF DRAPERY MANIA: PROTECTIVE LAYERS

Charles Frederick Worth's fashion house survived the turmoil that accompanied the change of power in 1870. Some of its former and international clients returned, and Worth continued down its chosen path.[25] The penchant for drapery that had started in the final years of the Second Empire was now in its heyday. Initially the drapery added fullness at the back of the dress skirt, with a combination of pleats and raised sections. All this was supported by a bustle,

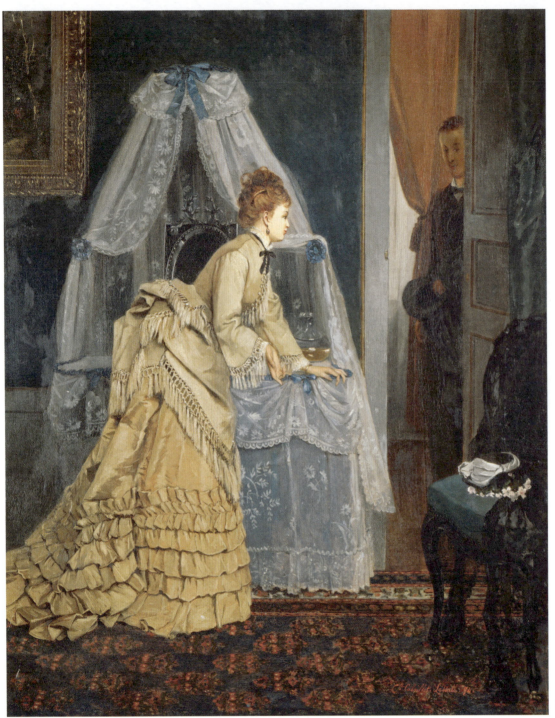

10 Camille-Léopold Lasalle, *The Vision*, oil on panel, 1874, Hinton Ampner, Ralph Dutton Collection, Hampshire, NT 1530132.
11 Detail of Fig. 13: C. Petit, afternoon dress in rep silk, embroidery and silk passementerie, The Hague, c. 1875, MoMu, Antwerp, T12/1312AB/J238.

12 Inside of a skirt with vertical boning channels and ties, c. 1885, MoMu, Antwerp, T12/316AB/J88.
13 C. Petit, afternoon dress in rep silk, embroidery and silk passementerie, The Hague, c. 1875. MoMu, Antwerp, T12/1312AB/J238.
14 Afternoon dress in plain and striped silk fabric, silk passementerie and glass beads, c. 1885, MoMu, Antwerp, T12/65AB/J89.
15 Eugène Maincent, design for an Oriental salon, hand-coloured lithograph, from *Le Garde-meuble ancien et moderne*, 1885-1895, Rijksmuseum Amsterdam, RP-P-2017-7591.
16 Eugène Maincent, design for a boudoir, hand-coloured lithograph, from *Le Garde-meuble ancien et moderne*, c. 1885-1895, Rijksmuseum Amsterdam, RP-P-2017-7543.

GRAND SALON, GENRE ORIENTAL

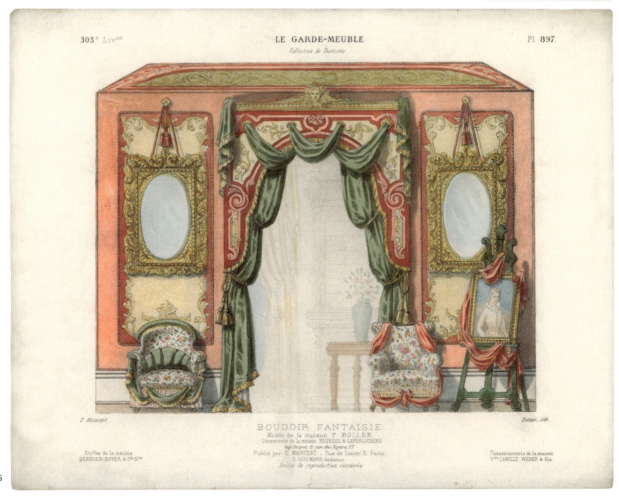

BOUDOIR FANTAISIE

SALON DE M. BLONDEL, ARCHITECTE, exécuté par la Société anonyme d'Ameublement, 26, avenue de l'Opéra.

17 Architect Blondel's salon, lithograph, 1883, Bibliothèque du Musée des Arts Décoratifs, Paris, Maciet 236/41.
18 Cartoon, lithograph, c. 1890.

a semi-circular whalebone construction introduced by Worth in the late 1860s and the successor of the cage crinoline.[26] The flat front of the dress was richly embellished with ruches, bands of embroidery and passementerie (Figs. 11 & 13). It was not unusual for different materials and textures to be combined. Around 1875, more and more draped panels resembling aprons and known as tabliers began to appear (Fig. 10). A draped shawl covering the skirt was an acceptable alternative.

The same trends were embraced inside the home, with drapes at the doors and the windows, combining layers of different fabrics finished with fringes, cords and tassels. Shawls were artfully draped over furniture.[27] Typical window and door embellishments consisted of a central swag flanked on either side by vertical pleated panels. They bear a striking resemblance to the tablier. This extravaganza of fabric at windows and doors, the entrances to the microworld of the family, was perceived as a protective shell against the noise, dirt and, by extension, dangers of the outside world.[28] The trauma of the repression of the Paris Commune in 1871 was still fresh in the collective memory. Fear of the plebs and of social unrest was rife among the bourgeoisie. Shielding the interior from prying eyes was further justification for dressing the windows with layers of drapery.

Parallel to this and in the context of the prevailing prudish bourgeois discourse, the plethora of drapes and embellishments on gowns, and on skirts in particular, could be seen as a protective shell, a defence. Indeed, according to Emmeline Raymond, editor of *La Mode illustrée*, it was most improper for the skirt to show the shape of the legs;[29] they were chastely concealed from view by drapery and embellishments.

After a short period of less ample draperies (1875-1882), around 1883 voluminous styles started to make a comeback: at the front in the tablier and at the back at the bustle. The latter gave the dress a more angular look than before. An innovation was the asymmetry, with the pleats or drapery falling differently on either side of the tablier or overskirt (Fig. 14). To ensure that the fall of the folds and drapery effects at the back of the skirt held their shape at all times, horizontal ribbons and/or horizontal tunnels were now created at regular intervals on the inside of the skirt. They contained whalebone stays which were tightened with ribbons to give and hold the desired shape (Fig. 12).

From that point on, the same asymmetry also dominated the interior. Even during the July Monarchy and the Second Empire, interiors flaunted furniture and all kinds of textile coverings, but some care was taken to arrange furniture symmetrically in general and to have matching textiles in each room, thus providing an air of serenity. As the century progressed, 'artistic' disarray with a touch of orientalism won favour (Fig. 15). Under the guise of good taste, seating and other items of furniture were arranged in a seemingly nonchalant manner and upholstered all over. In his book *An Illustrated History of Interior Decoration*, Mario Praz describes this as follows: 'The accessories, *petits riens*, the knick-knacks, the whimsical draperies (everything was draped: walls, fireplaces, mirrors, pianos, paintings on easels, flowerpots) finally became the protagonists of a décor',[30] as indeed the abundance of prints in upholsterers' manuals and journals of the time illustrate (Fig. 16). The upholsterers also benefitted from the wide range and availability of textiles which allowed them to make luxuriant window dressings and indulge in all manner of upholstered seating like the pouffe and the divan. Those seats, which were initially reserved for 'female' rooms such as the boudoir and the bedroom,[31] eventually also found their way into the salon. This was the least formal room in the house still open to the outside world and also the place where the lady of the house received visitors in the daytime.[32] In the evenings, the salon and dining room were the focus of the social life of both spouses. The wife's draped and embellished evening gowns, a reflection of the husband's success, resonated with the room's soft furnishings (Fig. 17).[33]

All this was in line with the male expectations of the time. In 1878, the Austrian cultural historian Jacob von Falke wrote that a lady should be in harmony with her surroundings; she should be 'the most beautiful ornament in her ornamented home'.[34] A British cartoon showed a woman dressed in a gown made from a medley of tablecloths and table runners in various styles, reflecting the mishmash inside the home (Fig. 18). If she was to sit on a divan, she would completely merge with her surroundings. Criticism of the excess of textiles nevertheless continued to build. Praz quoted Oscar Wilde: 'horrible things perpetrated in berlin wool, endless antimacassars… which seem to reduce life to the level of an eternal washing day.'[35] Though by the late 1880s, upholsterers were opting for a more sober style idiom and use of textiles, and preparing the way for 'the big clean-up',[36] the crammed interiors stood their ground, particularly among the middle classes. After 1890, the dust-gathering drapes gradually gave way, both in clothing and interior design.

Endnotes

1 Laure Chabanne, 'Luxe, mode et fantaisie. Le textile dans le décor intérieur,' in *Folie textile. Mode et décoration sous le Second Empire*, exh. cat. (Paris: Réunion des musées nationaux, 2013), 59.
2 Madeleine Deschamps, 'Domestic Elegance: The French at Home,' in *L'Art de vivre. Decorative Arts and Design in France 1789-1989*, exh. cat. (New York: The Vendome Press, 1989), 114–115.
3 Catherine Join-Diéterle, 'Revisiter le style Second Empire,' in *Sous l'Empire des crinolines*, exh. cat. (Paris: Paris-Musées, 2008), 19.
4 G.-Félix Lenoir, *Traité théorique et pratique du tapissier: principes de la décoration*, ed. Ch. Juliot (s.l.: s.n., 1893), 91. Designs for late-eighteenth-century neoclassical furniture and interiors also regularly feature drapery as embellishments. See, for example, the prints of Richard de Lalonde (1735–1808) and Pierre Ranson (1736–1786).
5 Chantal Trubert-Tollu et al., *The House of Worth, 1858-1954: The Birth of Haute Couture* (London: Thames & Hudson Ltd, 2017), 74.
6 Pastel hues were favourites, as were plain and striped fabrics embellished with ribbons, tassels and lace. Trubert-Tollu et al., *The House of Worth*, 75 and 79.
7 Join-Diéterle, 'Revisiter le style Second Empire,' 20.
8 Françoise Tétart-Vittu, 'Chez la couturière,' in *Folie textile. Mode et décoration sous le Second Empire*, exh. cat. (Paris: Réunion des musées nationaux, 2013), 48.
9 Trubert-Tollu, *The House of Worth*, 20–22.
10 Trubert-Tollu, 48–63.
11 Windows were dressed with combinations of heavy coloured curtains and white muslin sheers and crowned with a pelmet hung with a sober curtain drop or fringing. M. [Athanase] Garnier-Audiger, *Manuel du tapissier, décorateur, et marchand de meubles* (Paris: Librairie encyclopédique de Roret, 1830), 101.
12 Trubert-Tollu, *The House of Worth*, 96.
13 Marguerite Coppens, *Mode in België in de 19de eeuw* (Brussels: Friends of the Royal Museums of Art and History, 1996), 170.
14 This is beautifully illustrated in *The Morning Toilet* painted circa 1740 by the French artist Jean Siméon Chardin (1699–1779). A slit in the woman's overskirt allows her to access the pocket in her underskirt. By pulling the hem of the overskirt through the slit, she can keep it off the ground.
15 'Si vous lui (Eugénie) disiez qu'elle est belle, spirituelle, charitable, il est probable qu'elle ne vous répondrait pas. Mais si vous lui juriez que pas un tapissier ne s'y entend comme elle pour choisir des meubles, assortir des étoffes et décorer un salon. Elle me ferait peut-être décorer aussi?' Isabelle Dubois-Brinkmann and Emmanuel Starcky, introduction to *Folie textile. Mode et décoration sous le Second Empire*, by Anne-Rose Bringel et al., exh. cat. (Paris: Réunion des musées nationaux, 2013), 13–14.
16 Chabanne, 'Luxe, mode et fantaisie,' 57–58.
17 Deschamps, 'Domestic Elegance,' 114.
18 Stella Blum, *Victorian Fashions & Costumes from Harper's Bazar 1867-1898* (New York: Dover Publications, 1974), 3.
19 Initially the ladies' garments made in serial production and available in department stores were limited mainly to mantels and skirts. See Ykje Wildenborg, 'Naam gezocht voor nieuwe industrie. Confection, couture, prêt-à-porter,' *Studies in Textiel* 6 (2018), 21.
20 Beverly Gordon, 'Woman's Domestic Body: The Conceptual Conflation of Women and Interiors in the Industrial Age,' *Winterthur Portfolio*, 31, 4 (1996): 285, www.jstor.org/stable/1215239. In 1833 John Claudius Loudon wrote in his *Encyclopaedia* that curtain arranging was the perfect opportunity for a woman to display her taste. Peter Thornton, *L'époque et son style. La décoration intérieure 1620-1920*, trans. Jean-François Allain (Paris: Flammarion, 1986), 224.
21 Gordon, 'Woman's Domestic Body,' 285.
22 Chabanne, 'Luxe, mode et fantaisie,' 57.
23 The American magazine *The Delineator* (1869–1937) and *Godey's Lady's Book and Magazine* (1830–1898), for example, give not only detailed descriptions of ladies' and children's clothes, but also household tips.
24 Jennifer Grayer Moore, *Patternmaking History & Theory*, ed. Jennifer Grayer Moore (London – New York: Bloomsbury, 2020), 19–20. There was a considerable overlap between the patterns and instructions for creating drapes published in magazines and manuals, and their execution by seamstress/couturier or upholsterer respectively. The patterns looked the same, and the fabric panels were cut and the pleats folded in the same way.
25 Trubert-Tollu, *The House of Worth*, 94.
26 Trubert-Tollu, 99.
27 Gordon, 'Woman's Domestic Body,' 289. See also Dries Debackere's contribution in this book: 'A Woman's Most Versatile Fashion Accessory: The Reuse of Kashmir Shawls in Late nineteenth-Century Clothing and Interior Decoration', 32 et seq.
28 Deschamps, 'Domestic Elegance,' 116.
29 Coppens, *Mode in België*, 179.
30 Mario Praz, *An Illustrated History of Interior Decoration: From Pompeii to Art Nouveau* (London: Thames & Hudson, 1964), 65.
31 Chabanne, 'Luxe, mode et fantaisie,' 61.
32 Deschamps, 'Domestic Elegance,' 115–116.
33 Gordon, 'Woman's Domestic Body,' 286.
34 Gordon, 283.
35 Praz, *An Illustrated History of Interior Decoration: From Pompeii to Art Nouveau*, 65.
36 Thornton, *L'époque et son style*, 313.

20

19

19 Alfred Stevens, *Desperate*, 1873-1875, oil on panel, KMSKA, Antwerp, 1131.
20 Alfred Stevens, *The Cup of Tea*, 1878, oil on panel, Domaine & Musée royal de Mariemont, Morlanwelz.
21 Evening gown in tarlatan, silk satin and machine lace, 1865-1870, MoMu, Antwerp, T12/1248ABCD/J80.

1 Alfred Stevens, *La Visite*, pre-1869, oil on canvas, Dallas Museum of Art, gifted by the Pauline Allen Gill Foundation.

A WOMAN'S MOST VERSATILE FASHION ACCESSORY: THE REUSE OF KASHMIR SHAWLS IN LATE-NINETEENTH-CENTURY CLOTHING AND INTERIOR DECORATION

Dries Debackere

'Cloisonné enamels of wool', 'the wings of a Hindustan butterfly' and 'continents of turquoise, emerald and ruby'.[1] In 1899, the French author and aristocrat Robert de Montesquiou (1855-1921) used these fantastical terms to describe the Kashmir shawls which had so captivated the West in the nineteenth century. Fashionable ladies coveted these shawls for their rich colour palette, softness, warmth and evocation of the East. Initially they were imported, but soon European manufacturers – like Frédéric Hébert in France – began to produce high-quality imitations (Fig. 2).[2] Both Indian and European Kashmir shawls were considered luxury items and, therefore, a symbol of status and respectability.[3]

In *La visite*, for example, the Belgian artist Alfred Stevens (1823-1906) depicted two wealthy ladies in a sumptuously decorated interior (Fig. 1). One of them is wearing a *déshabillé* made of pink silk and a transparent white fabric embellished with frills and insertions. As this kind of garment was only appropriate in the domestic sphere, it indicates that the wearer is the lady of the house. The lady on the right is paying her a visit. She is wearing a hat, gloves and a Kashmir shawl adorned with tassels which is draped around her like a cloak. A fashion plate from the French magazine *Revue de la mode* (1872-1913) depicts two similarly dressed women in what could be seen as a sequel to Stevens's painting (Fig. 3). The hostess is wearing a *matinée* – a type of *déshabillé* consisting of a bodice and matching skirt – made of pink silk and trimmed with lace. Next to her is a woman in a brown *toilette d'intérieur*, suggesting that she too is part of the household. Both women appear to have just escorted a visitor into the hall. As in Stevens's painting, the latter wears a hat and a Kashmir shawl as part of her *toilette de visite*. This ensemble was intended for the public sphere, where the shawl served as a clear indication of the wearer's affluence.

At the beginning of the twentieth century, Montesquiou lamented that these 'feminine textile jewels' were now only to be seen on the shoulders of the women depicted by Stevens.[4] Indeed, from 1870 onwards, the Kashmir shawl had gradually fallen out of favour as an accessory due to the emergence of a new fashion silhouette. In contrast to the delicate Empire dresses of the early nineteenth century and the wide mid-century crinoline skirts, it was difficult to elegantly drape a Kashmir shawl over the sharply protruding bustle that characterised the new silhouette.[5] Late-nineteenth-century fashion magazines nevertheless continued to describe the shawl as 'in good taste' and 'essentially aristocratic'. Like Montesquiou's florid words, this illustrates that the Kashmir shawl still stood for affluence, elegance and respectability.[6] Consequently, in their reluctance to relinquish this once coveted accessory, women started reusing it in different ways.

Kashmir shawls were very large – often more than one-and-a-half metres wide and over three metres long – so they came to be seen as a 'rich fabric by the metre' for making items of clothing.[7] This meant that an old shawl could be turned into a *pardessus* or overcoat. These were elegantly trimmed with passementerie in shades that closely matched the nuances of the shawl. An example is a *visite* made by Maison Cavally in Paris, embellished with a colourful fringe of silk chenille and cord, embroidered buttons, and frogging on the back (Fig. 6). Such jackets prolonged the life of the Kashmir shawl as a garment to be worn outdoors,

2 Frédéric Hébert, Kashmir wool shawl, 1850-1860, MoMu, Antwerp, T02/298AB.
3 A. Chaillot, print from *Revue de la mode*, 1880, Vol. 9, No. 423, private collection.

4 Dressing gown in woven wool fabric with Kashmir motifs, 1878-1890, MoMu, Antwerp, T12/374/J219.
5 Tea gown remodelled from a Kashmir shawl, c. 1891, The Metropolitan Museum of Art, New York, acquisition, Irene Lewisohn and Alice L. Crowley Bequests, 1985, inv. 1985.39.3.
6 Maison Cavally, jacket in woven wool fabric with Kashmir motifs, silk and chenille fringing, 1875-1885, Paris, MoMu, Antwerp, T12/108/M27.
7 & 8 Mme Haussemberg, dressing gown remodelled from a Kashmir shawl, from *La mode illustrée*, No. 45, 10 November 1878, Paris, Ville de Paris, Bibliothèque Forney.

in the public sphere, where they were an abiding reminder of the wearer's status.

Kashmir shawls were also reused indoors. For example, ladies would have their old shawl transformed into a *robe d'intérieur* or interior gown. This type of garment was often looser and more comfortable than those intended for the public sphere. The bodice of a dressing gown in the MoMu collection (Fig. 4), for example, is not stiffened with whalebone, which indicates that it was intended to be worn without a corset or at least with a looser variation, a so-called *corset de repos* (resting corset) or *corset de maison* (house corset). This was only appropriate in the privacy of the home, when one was alone or in the company of family members or close acquaintances.

In 1878 the French fashion magazine *La mode illustrée* (1860-1937) featured a similar dressing gown (Figs. 7 & 8). It was made of a plain cashmere fabric onto which teardrop-shaped motifs and borders cut from a Kashmir shawl were appliquéd. This technique was another way of breathing new life into outmoded and especially damaged shawls, and was applied to both outerwear and at-home wear. Cutting out, artistically arranging and, above all, reattaching the motifs with embroidery stitches that imitate the weave of the shawl required considerable skill. Hence the advice of fashion journalists Coralie L. and Emmeline Raymond to leave such transformations to seamstresses like Mme Turpin and Mme Haussemberg in Paris, who specialised in repairing and adapting Kashmir shawls.[8]

Other interior gowns made from Kashmir shawls had a closer-fitting bodice and were meant to be worn with a corset. This made them more formal and thus suitable for wearing in front of a wider

7

8

audience, for example at the *jour de réception* held by the lady of the house. This was a fixed afternoon in the week on which she received visitors at home in the salon. During the Belle Époque, these daytime receptions were an important way of strengthening the family's social network, and the clothes worn by the hostess could play a role in this. Some women, therefore, chose to wear a luxurious interior gown known as a tea gown – so named because of the tea and refreshments the hostess would serve. As a tea gown was often inspired by historical or non-Western dress, an old Kashmir shawl was a suitable material for making this type of interior gown.[9] Instead of the visitor wrapped in her Kashmir shawl in Stevens's *La Visite*, in this context it could be the hostess whose elegant tea gown (Fig. 5) defined her as a respectable lady of standing.

The décor of the salon in which a lady received her guests also had a role to play in communicating her status and good taste. During the Belle Époque, interiors were decorated with many different textiles, and here too the connotations of the Kashmir shawl could be relied upon to create an atmosphere of affluence, respectability and elegance. Fashion journalists encouraged their readers to attach the borders of old Kashmir shawls to a plain textile to make a large *tapis de table*, or to use fragments to make smaller table cloths, for example edged with gold passementerie (Fig. 9).[10] An appliqué embroidery of Kashmir fragments could also be used to make a cushion, a pouf or an antimacassar (a piece of cloth placed over the back of an armchair). Like an overcoat made from a Kashmir shawl, these decorative objects were embellished with colourful passementerie in the same shades as the shawl.[11]

Intact Kashmir shawls were also eagerly used to decorate the interior. While these shawls were still at the forefront of fashion, a number of artists already depicted ladies who had nonchalantly thrown their shawl onto an armchair. This confirmed the decorative qualities of the colourful textile and almost seemed to predict its repurposing in the late-nineteenth- and early-twentieth-century home. Indeed, in that period they were used as *portières* and window curtains, or artistically draped over sofas and pianos, as seen in the portrait of a young woman in a salon, with a Kashmir shawl knotted onto the back of the piano behind her (Fig. 10).[12]

Complete shawls were also used as *tapis de table* or table cloths, as in *Intérieur* or *Le goûter* by the French artist Maurice Lobre (1862-1951).[13] The 1888 painting depicts a young girl sitting at a round table which is draped in a red Kashmir shawl. An older woman, possibly her grandmother, is adding milk to a cup of tea. The room is soberly furnished with simple chairs, plain walls, and sparse decoration. In the contemporary publication *Salon illustré* (1888-1894), the French art critic Roger Ballu (1852-1908) described it as 'a very simple apartment, probably on the fourth or fifth floor'.[14] The girl and the old woman are part of the middle class – not the aristocracy or upper-middle class as represented by Stevens – which indicates that the repurposing of Kashmir shawls for interior decoration was widespread.

Although Kashmir shawls were no longer fashionable as accessories during the last decades of the nineteenth century, women found ways of reusing these – in the words of De Montesquiou – 'kaleidoscopic woven gems'.[15] They were taken apart and transformed into

9   Table runner made from a Kashmir shawl, passementerie, 1800-1900, MoMu, Antwerp, T08/114.
10 c. 1890, Musée de Photographie Charleroi, MPC 96/332. Joseph Joudain, portrait of a young woman,

garments for indoor or outdoor wear, as well as into decorative objects for the home, thus continuing to serve as a symbol of affluence, respectability and good taste. The many different ways in which Kashmir shawls were repurposed allowed them to transcend the boundary between fashionable clothing and interior decoration, in the process also showing just how closely the two were linked.

Endnotes

1 _____ Robert de Montesquiou, 'Alfred Stevens,' *Le Figaro* (November 11, 1899): 1.
2 _____ Monique Lévi-Strauss, *Cachemires parisiens à l'école de l'Asie, 1810-1880* (Paris: Paris Musées, 1998), 85–86.
3 _____ Madeleine Delpierre, 'Le châle cachemire et la mode française,' in *La mode du châle cachemire en France*, Monique Lévi-Strauss, Frédérique Delbecq and Madeleine Delpierre (Paris: Paris Musées, 1982), 29–33; Michelle Maskiell, 'Consuming Kashmir. Shawls and Empires, 1500-2000,' *Journal of World History* 13, No. 1 (2002): 35, 39; Susan Hiner, *Accessories to Modernity. Fashion and the Feminine in Nineteenth-Century France* (Philadelphia: University of Pennsylvania Press, 2010), 82–84.
4 _____ Robert de Montesquiou, *Diptyque de Flandre. Triptyque de France* (Paris: Éditions E. Sansot, 1921), 21–23.
5 _____ Delpierre, 'Châle cachemire,' 33–34; Janet Rizvi, 'The Kashmir Shawl and Its Use in the Indo-Islamic World and Europe,' in *Berg Encyclopedia of World Dress and Fashion. South Asia and Southeast Asia*, ed. Jasleen Dhamija (Oxford: Bloomsbury, 2010), 169.
6 _____ Agnès Verboom, 'Courrier de la mode,' *Journal des dames et des demoiselles* (November 15, 1876): 18; Marguerite de Colombes, 'Revue critique des modes,' *Journal des dames et des demoiselles* (July 1, 1879): 331; Marguerite de Colombes, 'Revue critique des modes,' *Journal des dames et des demoiselles* (October 1, 1879): 451.
7 _____ Emmeline Raymond, 'Transformation des châles de cachemire de l'Inde,' *La mode illustrée* (September 24, 1882): 310.

8 _____ Emmeline Raymond, 'Modes. Emploi des pointes de dentelle et des châles de cachemire,' *La mode illustrée* (May 16, 1875): 157; Raymond, 'Transformation des châles,' 310; Coralie L., 'Modes,' *Journal des demoiselles* (December 12, 1874): 3; Coralie L., 'Transformation des anciens châles de cachemire de l'Inde en sortie de bal ou en robe de chambre, Maison Turpin, rue de Châteaudun, 19,' *Journal des demoiselles* (January 16, 1875): 3.
9 _____ Valerie Steele, *Fashion and Eroticism. Ideals of Feminine Beauty from the Victorian Era to the Jazz Age* (Oxford: Oxford University Press, 1985), 209–10; Valerie Steele, *Paris Fashion. A Cultural History*, 3rd imp. (London: Bloomsbury, 2017), 157, 167–68; Anne Bissonnette, 'Victorian Tea Gowns. A Case of High Fashion Experimentation,' *Dress. The Journal of the Costume Society of America* 44, No. 1 (2018): 3–8, 25.
10 _____ Emmeline Raymond, 'Décors. Ameublement. Travaux relatifs à l'ameublement,' *La mode illustrée* (June 11, 1876): 190.
11 _____ Emmeline Raymond, 'Ameublement,' *La mode illustrée* (February 18, 1877): 51–54; 'Application de cretonne pour tapis, chaise, pouf, coussin, etc.,' *Journal des dames et des demoiselles* (October 15, 1883): 286–87.
12 _____ Raymond, 'Décors,' 190; Emmeline Raymond, 'Pêle-mêle. Nouveautés,' *La mode illustrée* (May 1881): 150.
13 _____ Raymond, 'Pêle-mêle,' 150.
14 _____ Roger Ballu, 'Salon de 1889,' in *Salon illustré* (Paris: Librairie d'art Ludovic Baschet, 1889), 14.
15 _____ Montesquiou, *Diptyque/Triptyque*, 22.

Richard Malone, chair made of draped econyl (78% recycled polyester, 22% elastane), 2025.
Malone creates installations, sculptures, furniture and clothing, intuitively applying such skills as sewing, draping, metal- and wood-working. As a working-class queer from rural Ireland, he/they reflect on the gender and class connotations of these techniques throughout their practice.

Richard Malone, recycled deadstock jersey dress, with wooden dowels and tailoring canvas underneath, Spring-Summer 2022.

WEARING THE HOME IN TIMES OF TROUBLE

Romy Cockx

Over the last two decades, elements from the home – ranging from bedding through carpets to chairs – have been integrated into fashion silhouettes by fashion designers. What may sometimes appear to be gimmicky creations reflect the precarious situation of a modern Western ideal: the house as a 'home', a place where comfort, safety, privacy and domesticity converge.

The seed of this concept was sown in the seventeenth-century Netherlands, where the home acquired a new sense of a private space and the middle-class wife was responsible for the housekeeping.[1] For most Europeans at that time, the dwelling was where work and relaxation were shared with a wide social network of family and live-in employees. The concept of domestic 'comfort' only took root under the reign of King Louis XV (1710-1774). From then on, an unprecedented assortment of upholstered and stuffed seating accommodated the refined manners and dress style of the French aristocracy.[2] During the nineteenth century, accelerated industrialization and urbanization brought privacy, domesticity and comfort within reach of a growing middle class. The home became a sanctuary for the husband who went out to work. His wife stayed at home, and her taste in both fashion and interior decoration reflected the family's social status.[3] Today we can no longer take cover behind our drapery. Hence the suggestion of some fashion designers that we wear home comforts outdoors.

BEDDING AND HOME TEXTILES AS ARMOUR

In the run-up to the year 2000, there was real concern about the 'millennium bug', which it was believed would cause computer systems around the world to fail, possibly resulting in power outages, plane crashes and an apocalyptic recession. Thanks to Maison Martin Margiela, women could prepare for the worst and take the comfort of a warm bed with them wherever they went. The Maison's Autumn-Winter 1999-2000 collection featured a white coat made out of a duvet: two long removable sleeves attached with zips to a quilted, feather-filled, cotton duvet. The Maison presented the collection in a film in which vintage floral motifs were projected onto the models wearing the white coat (Fig. 5) so that they seemed to merge with the wallpaper. Ringing out in the background was Timmy Thomas's song 'Why Can't We Live Together'. The duvet coat could be worn with a cover made from 1970s floral bedsheets (Fig. 4) or with a protective PVC cover.

Simultaneously with Margiela, Walter Van Beirendonck designed several blanket coats for men (Autumn-Winter 1999-2000 collection). A quilt consisting of patches of printed cotton fabrics was secured around the body with a cord and a safety pin (Fig. 7). The frayed edge revealed a warm lining and underneath a bodysuit. Van Beirendonck sent his models confidently into the new millennium in protective gear: they wore helmets designed to protect them from sunlight and the atmosphere.[4]

Wearing bedroom comforts has since been explored by numerous fashion designers. For example, the Dutch designer duo Viktor & Rolf added satin pillows to a collection that merged evening wear and sleep wear with bedding (Autumn-Winter 2005-2006 collection) (Fig. 6). The luxury materials, finished with embroidery and lace, and the title *Bedtime Story* evoked the atmosphere of an escapist dream from which you never want to wake up. *Vogue* suggested: 'Why not go out to work in your bed?',[5] a notion that ties in with the ascertainment that the gendered distinction between private and public prevalent during the nineteenth century no longer exists today. We live in a 24/7 culture from which the rigid separation

1   John Galliano for Maison Margiela, trompe l'œil Chesterfield-printed dress, transparent coat, bolster and backpack with integrated screen, Autumn-Winter 2018-2019, Artisanal Collection.

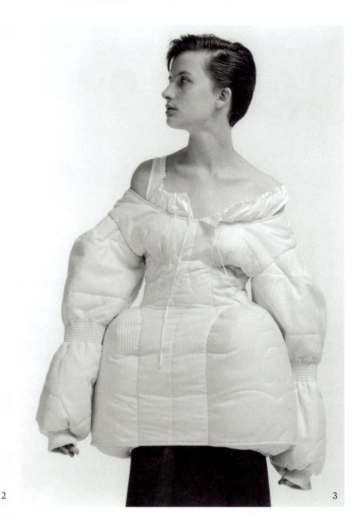

2   Simone Rocha, bomber jacket inspired by vintage eiderdowns, Spring-Summer 2023, MoMu, Antwerp, X2150.
3   Marine Serre, deadstock blanket couture dress, Autumn-Winter 2019-2020, photographed by Valeria Herklotz for *Dazed*.
4   Maison Martin Margiela, duvet coat with flower-printed cover, Autumn-Winter 1999-2000, MoMu, Antwerp, X1443.
5   Maison Martin Margiela, duvet coat with floral overlay, Autumn-Winter 1999-2000, photographed by Marina Faust.

Grand châle en maille laine & lurex REF:31A036. Duvet long REF:732506. Jupe rayures tennis en laine REF:31N109. // Big knitted shawl in wool & lurex REF:31A036. Long duvet REF:732506. Pinstriped wool skirt REF:31N109.

6   Viktor & Rolf, duvet coat in quilted silk satin with embroidered pillows, Autumn-Winter 2005-2006, photographed by David LaChapelle, *House at the End of the World*, 2005.

7   Walter Van Beirendonck, long coat made from a patchwork quilt, Autumn-Winter 1999-2000, MoMu, Antwerp. X1556.

8   Jenny Fax, pillowcase mini-skirt with pillow apron, Autumn-Winter 2022-2023, MoMu, Antwerp. X2004.

9   Comme des Garçons, quilted floral-printed dress, Spring-Summer 2020, photographed by Elizaveta Porodina for *Magazine*, No. 37, Spring-Summer 2022.

between work, leisure, domesticity and sleep has been removed.[6]

With the Tokyo-based label Jenny Fax, pillows and pillowcases took on the shape of the body (Autumn-Winter 2022-2023 collection) (Fig. 8). The Taiwanese designer Jen-Fang Shueh turned bedding from an ultra-girly teenager's bedroom into soft armour. The pillow is no longer a pillow to drift off to sleep on but one that helps you face the world.

The collections of Marine Serre, who like Shueh studied at La Cambre, regularly feature repurposed home textiles, including constants like silhouettes made out of sheets, blankets (Fig. 3) and table linen. She also gives brocade home furnishing fabrics a new lease of life. In her 2020 Autumn-Winter collection, she combined them with her signature crescent-moon motif, jeans and a vision of the future in which people are able to travel between planets (Fig. 11).[7] Craig Green sent 'carpets' strutting down the runway. His creations often feature architectural volumes, creating a seemingly protective environment. A sense of isolation provides recurring inspiration, and in his Autumn-Winter collection for 2017-2018 this was expressed in clothes that enabled the wearer to brave unfamiliar waters and an uncertain future (Fig. 10).[8] Both designers encourage us to go on a journey of discovery in their wearable home textiles.

WALKING FURNITURE

Travel, nomadism and displacement are also important themes in the work of Hussein Chalayan: 'Our lives are in a constant state of mobility and [...] in some ways that could affect memory, could effect our attachment to domestic things. What would new comfort zones be in those kinds of situations? You know it's this whole idea of creating a refuge wherever you are.'[9] He has frequently explored the borders between fashion and furniture design, and in a number of respects his *Afterwords* collection (Autumn-Winter 2000-2001) (Figs. 22 & 23), was trailblazing. During his show, the models entered an all-white space furnished with four chairs, a coffee table, a flatscreen television and a selection of vases and bowls which, one by one, they picked up and took with them. At the end of the show, four of the models removed the covers from the chairs. They then put the covers on over their grey shift dresses, two of the covers having first been turned inside out. The chairs were folded up

10 Craig Green, garments in rug-like textiles, Autumn-Winter 2017-2018, photographed backstage by Morgan O'Donovan.
11 Marine Serre, recycled tablecloth top, Autumn-Winter 2020-2021.

12 Maison Margiela, T-shirt dress featuring Mariano Fortuny interior-design fabric panels, Spring-Summer 2014, Artisanal Collection, photographed by Willy Vanderperre for System, #3, 2014.
13 Walter Van Beirendonck, suit sporting inwoven parquet motif, wallpaper and painting, Spring-Summer 2014, MoMu, Antwerp, X238.
14 Dirk Van Saene, overalls with floral wallpaper apron, Spring-Summer 2000, MoMu, Antwerp, X410l.
15 Dries Van Noten, jacket with wallpaper print and knitted shorts, Spring-Summer 2017, MoMu, Antwerp, X80l.

13

14

15

16 Chalayan, dress with neck support, Autumn-Winter 2006-2007.
17 Charlotte Perriand seated on her swivel chair B302, c. 1930, Charlotte Perriand Archives.
18 Charlotte Perriand reclining on the B306 chaise longue, which she designed with Le Corbusier and Pierre Jeanneret, 1928 or 1929, Charlotte Perriand Archives.

into suitcases. The last model stepped inside the coffee table and transformed it into a wooden skirt. Chalayan was referencing the experiences of refugees hastily packing up their belongings as they are forced to flee. Not only was this a topical theme at the time, following in the wake of the war in Kosovo (1998-1999), but it was also personal to the Turkish-Cypriot designer who had had to flee his homeland in the 1970s.[10]

Once again, Chalayan incorporated home furniture into his *Repose* collection (Autumn-Winter 2006-2007). This time as an invitation to take a break, no matter where. He appeared to be leading the audience in reverse through the history of the modern Western interior, opening the show with several short black dresses whose round leather collars (Fig. 16) are reminiscent of Charlotte Perriand's 1927 swivel chair, her *fauteuil pivotant* (Fig. 17). These were followed by dresses with Art Nouveau necklines that brought to mind garments Henry van de Velde designed for his wife Maria. Finally, a number of quilted-velvet silhouettes referenced an upholstery method common in the Victorian era, when it was considered that a woman's proper and only place was in the home.

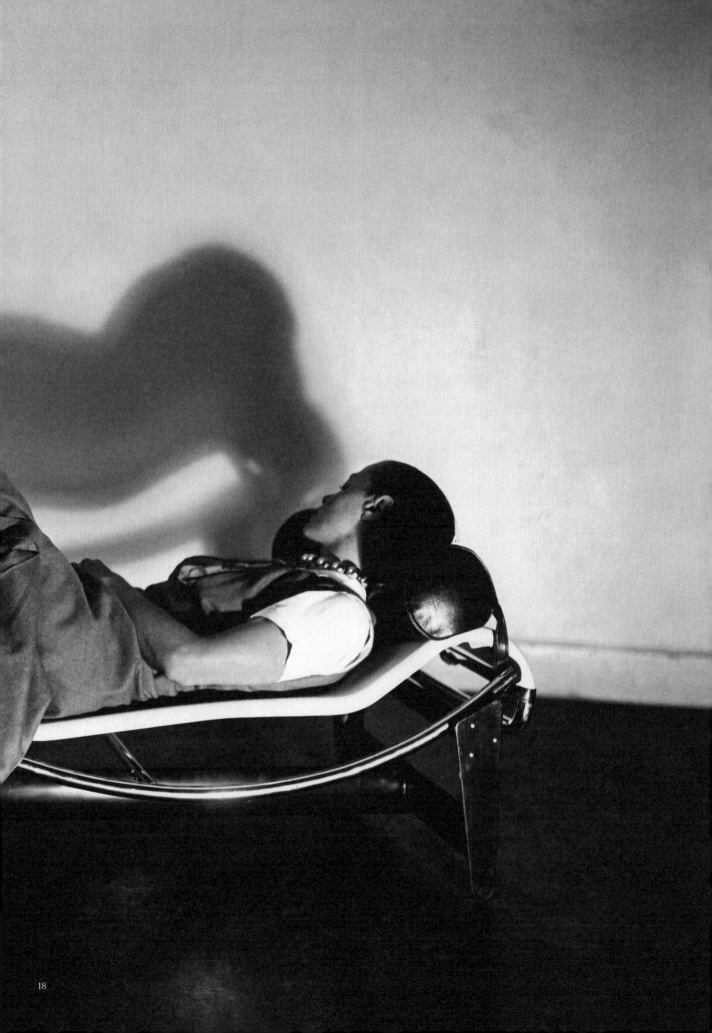

19 Maison Martin Margiela, leather seat-cover jacket, Autumn-Winter 2006-2007.
20 Maison Martin Margiela, sleeveless top with armchair print and skirt made from seat cover, Autumn-Winter 2006-2007.
21 Bernhard Willhelm, padded leather bomber jacket featuring deep buttoning, Autumn-Winter 2005-2006, MoMu, Antwerp. X520.

That same season (Autumn-Winter 2006-2007), Maison Martin Margiela also merged fashion and furniture, remodelling seat covers into clothing. The collection included a jacket made using the leather upholstery from an easy chair (Fig. 19) and also a velvet skirt using recycled material from an armchair (Fig. 20). Large sales tags listing the specifications were attached to the clothes or printed on white T-shirts. Upholstery nails adorned hems and seams, and the remote control for an electric reclining chair served as a belt.

Besides translating his interest in deconstruction and repurposing into furniture, Margiela also used it to indulge his penchant for trompe l'oeils. Several items of clothing in the Autumn-Winter 2004-2005 collection were screen-printed with the padded leather of a Chesterfield armchair (Fig. 21, p. 203) or a rattan seat. The collection was presented to the press in a film in which the models, located in different interiors, speak in voice-overs. A double trompe l'oeil was created because they sat on furniture which they wore printed on their body while talking about themselves, their memories and fears. Woman and furniture became one, and the interior served as an extension of the soul with the effect that the collection unconsciously evoked a nineteenth-century ideal.[11]

John Galliano had been designing for Maison Margiela for four years when he took up the Chesterfield theme in 2018 (Autumn-Winter couture collection). He presented it in a layered silhouette together with a trench coat knotted around the head. A rucksack consisting of a pillow, yoga bolster and screen provided the nomadic wearer with a few comforting mod cons (Fig. 1). As with his controversial *Clochard* collection (for Christian Dior Spring-Summer 2002), Galliano found inspiration in people 'who choose not to live within the confines of society', who dress in layers with 'their most precious possessions on them'. He felt the need to create 'his own world within a world that is currently very troubled'.[12]

Though the physical comfort of the average Westerner's home is greater than ever today, the incessant news bulletins and social-media messages invading our living rooms and bedrooms constantly confront us with the fragility of an elusive concept. The ever-increasing stream of refugees is fuelling a frenetic defence of this ideal. Climate change has also led to a growing realization that we don't know where we will find safety and comfort in the long term. We suppress our awareness that privacy is now a thing of the past with a quick click of the mouse in our hunger for even more information and material possessions. Fashion reflects these contradictions and fears. Perhaps Botter's 2022 Autumn-Winter collection can help us embrace uncertainty? Inspired by the Caribbean culture, the fashion duo created light-weight, fake-fur-covered chairs which can be taken anywhere for an honest, human-to-human conversation (Figs. 24 & 25).

22

Endnotes

1 ⎯⎯⎯ The number of servants was restricted by Dutch law. See Witold Rybczynski, *Home: A Short History of an Idea* (New York: Penguin Books, 1986), 72.
2 ⎯⎯⎯ According to Rybczynski, this development can largely be explained by aristocratic women wanting less formality and by the space required to accommodate their voluminous skirts. Hence, too, the names given to different types of seats, like the *marquise* and the *duchesse*. Rybczynski, *Home: A Short History of an Idea*, 94–95.
3 ⎯⎯⎯ Penny Sparke, *As Long as It's Pink: The Sexual Politics of Taste* (Halifax: The Press of the Nova Scotia College, 2010), XXI, 13.
4 ⎯⎯⎯ Luc Derycke, *Belgian Fashion Design*, ed. Sandra Van de Veire (Ludion: Ghent-Amsterdam, 1999), 143.
5 ⎯⎯⎯ Sarah Mower, 'Viktor & Rolf, Fall 2005,' *Vogue* (March 2, 2005) www.vogue.com/fashion-shows/fall-2005-ready-to-wear/viktor-rolf.
6 ⎯⎯⎯ Beatriz Colomina, 'The 24/7 Bed: Privacy and Publicity in the Age of Social Media,' in *How to Relate: Knowledge, Arts, Practices*, eds. Annika Haas, Maximilian Haas, Hanna Magauer and Dennis Pohl (Bielefeld: transcript Verlag, 2021), 186.
7 ⎯⎯⎯ 'Mind Mélange Motor,' Marine Serre website, accessed November 22, 2024, www.marineserre.com/show/mind-melange-motor. Serre reports that the textiles come from all over the world 'with no fear of travel': 'Core Values,' Marine Serre website, accessed November 22, 2024, core.marineserre.com/regenerated/carpets/.
8 ⎯⎯⎯ Suzanne Madsen, 'Craig Green reveals the meaning of his anonymous travellers,' *Dazed* (January 17, 2017) www.dazeddigital.com/fashion/article/34217/1/craig-green-on-the-meaning-behind-his-anonymous-travellers-aw17-interview.
9 ⎯⎯⎯ Hussein Chalayan in conversation with Marcus Fairs, *Icon* (December 1993) quoted by Caroline Evans, 'No Man's Land,' in *Hussein Chalayan*, ed. Caroline Evans (Rotterdam: NAi, 2005), 13.
10 ⎯⎯⎯ Caroline Evans, *Fashion at the Edge: Spectacle, Modernity and Deathliness* (New Haven and London: Yale University Press, 2003), 288.
11 ⎯⎯⎯ See Beverly Gordon, 'Woman's Domestic Body. The Conceptual Conflation of Women and Interiors in the Industrial Age,' *Winterthur Portfolio*, winter 1996, vol. 31, No. 4, 281–301.
12 ⎯⎯⎯ John Galliano quoted by Hamish Bowles, 'Maison Margiela, Fall Couture 2018,' *Vogue* (July 4, 2018) www.vogue.com/fashion-shows/fall-2018-couture/maison-martin-margiela.

22 Chalayan, transformation of armchair covers into dresses, Autumn-Winter 2000-2001.
23 Chalayan, transformation of a coffee table into a skirt, Autumn-Winter 2000-2001.

24 Botter, faux-fur upcycled Monobloc chair, Autumn-Winter 2022-2023, photographed backstage by Elie Benistant.
25 Botter, faux-fur upcycled Monobloc chair, Autumn-Winter 2022-2023, photographed by Thibaut Grevet for *SSAW, AW 22*.

'The application of the principles of rational design to a woman's wardrobe was part of my attempt to find a fresh approach to creating objects for everyday use'

'L'application des principes de la conception rationnelle à la toilette rentrait dans le cadre de l'action que je menais pour donner à la création d'objets d'usage quotidien un nouveau point de départ, valable pour l'ensemble de cette production.'
(Henry van de Velde, *Récit de ma vie*, 1863-1900, 375)

Maria Sèthe in a house dress, sitting in an armchair designed by Henry van de Velde in the dining room at Villa Bloemenwerf, c. 1900, La Fondation L'Écuyer, Brussels.

1 Maria Sèthe and her three children in the garden at Villa Bloemenwerf, photographed by Emile Tassel and Charles Lefébure, c. 1900, KBR depot at AML, Brussels, FSI0 00192/0882/011.

2 Maria Sèthe in a tea gown designed by Henry van de Velde, photographed by Emile Tassel and Charles Lefébure, c. 1900, KBR depot at AML, Brussels, FSI0 01039/0882/004.

3 Maria Sèthe in a tea gown designed by Henry van de Velde, photographed by Emile Tassel and Charles Lefébure, c. 1900, KBR depot at AML, Brussels, FSI0 00882/0001/002/12.

HENRY VAN DE VELDE'S METAMORPHOSIS: VILLA BLOEMENWERF AND THE ROLE OF HENRY'S MUSE MARIA SÈTHE

Werner Adriaenssens

Belgian artist Henry van de Velde (1863-1957) produced a cross-disciplinary body of work which includes paintings, graphics, typography, book art, designs for furniture and interiors, and also architecture. As well as a visionary designer, he was also an influential theorist whose work was infused with social engagement. A lesser-known aspect of his oeuvre is the clothing he designed with his wife Maria Sèthe in the setting of their home, Villa Bloemenwerf. Although she invariably stayed in the background, Maria was an indispensable partner and pillar of support in Van de Velde's artistic development.

THE INFLUENCE OF THE ARTS AND CRAFTS MOVEMENT AND OF SOCIAL CONTACTS ON VAN DE VELDE'S ARTISTIC TRAJECTORY

In a radical artistic departure, between 1892 and 1894 Henry van de Velde's focus shifted from painting to the applied arts. Crucial in this was his encounter with the Belgian painter William Finch at the *Les XX* Salon in 1892. Finch introduced Van de Velde, who had trained as an artist, to the thinking of John Ruskin and William Morris, prominent figures in the British Arts and Crafts movement. This led to a profound change in Henry's perception of art, in which the artistic and decorative crafts came to occupy a central role.[1] After much hesitation, in February 1893 Henry van de Velde exhibited a piece of embroidery titled *Engelenwake* (The Angels' Watch) at the final *Les XX* Salon. This was an important step; from that point on, he regarded himself as an artisan. Several months later, he met the young pianist and artist Maria Sèthe through one of his friends, the painter Théo Van Rysselberghe (Fig. 14). During a walk in Zeeland, Maria asked him about his artistic change of direction. Though irritated by her direct questions, Van de Velde opened up for the first time and told her about the influence of John Ruskin and William Morris on his work, and about his aspiration to follow their ideals.[2] That conversation, on his thirtieth birthday, was liberating, and his artistic uncertainties gradually began to recede. Maria was well informed about developments in the applied arts in England[3] and offered to collect documentation about the Arts and Crafts movement during the trip she was planning to London. He gave her specific instructions about companies and artists he was interested in – among them William Morris – wallpaper manufacturers and publishers of art books.[4] She had a good command of English and would also translate important treatises into French for him.[5] This enabled Henry to explore and gain a more in-depth understanding of the innovative British artistic movement. Maria's cultural background, artistic affinities and creative talent were of crucial importance in the evolution of her husband-to-be.

MARIA SÈTHE'S ROLE IN HENRY VAN DE VELDE'S ARTISTIC WORK

During his professorship at the National Higher Institute of Fine Arts in Antwerp, which began in 1893, Henry was able to develop and share his ideas on the decorative arts. As he gradually turned his back on the 'art for art's sake' doctrine, he emphasised the importance of applied art being accessible to everyone.[6] His first articles were devoted to the subject of wallpaper. In his teaching notes, he twice refers to the *papier Sèthe*, illustrated with a sketch which later became known as the 'Dahlia' wallpaper (Fig. 6).[7] The use of the term *papier Sèthe* suggests that Maria may have been the sole author of this design. In his memoirs, however, Van de Velde is less explicit. On the one hand, he mentions that Maria and he created their best wallpapers together, but he also states that the designs for both 'Dahlia' and the second wallpaper, 'Tulipes' (Fig. 4), were entirely Maria's work.[8]

This ambiguity in his memoirs, written decades after the events, can be explained

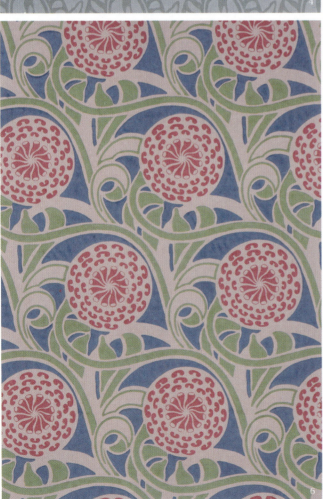

4 Maria Sèthe and Henry van de Velde (?), 'Tulipes' wallpaper, 1893, KIK-IRPA, Brussels.
5 Henry van de Velde, bookcase in Irma Sèthe's salon with the 'Tulipes' wallpaper, from *Dekorative Kunst*, 1898, KMKG-MRAH, Brussels.
6 Maria Sèthe, 'Dahlia' wallpaper, 1893, Nordenfjeldske Kunstindustrimuseum, Trondheim.

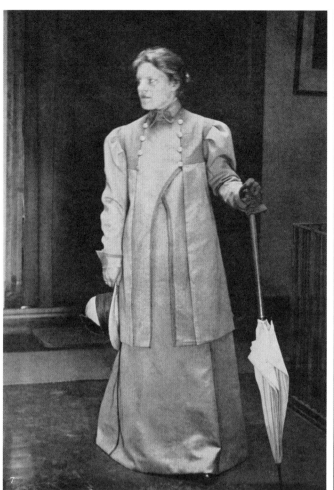

7   Maria Sèthe on the mezzanine floor at Bloememwerf in a town dress designed by Henry van de Velde, c. 1900, from *Album Robes de Dames*, 1900, plate 8, KMKG-MRAH, Brussels.
8   Maria Sèthe in the central hall at Bloemenwerf in an evening gown designed by Henry van de Velde, c. 1898, from *Album Robes de Dames*, 1900, plate 10, KMKG-MRAH, Brussels.
9   Maria Sèthe in the atelier on the ground floor at Bloemenwerf, photographed by Emile Tassel and Charles Lefébure, c. 1900, KBR depot at AML, Brussels, FS10 00882/0001/002/15.

by the contrast between the floral patterns of the early designs and the later abstract and linear style that would come to typify Van de Velde. Maria Sèthe, who was passionately fond of flowers, drew them regularly, including dahlias. It is probable that either the couple or Henry alone developed one of her drawings to create the 'Dahlia' pattern.[9]

According to sources, Henry van de Velde integrated into his first interior design the 'Tulipes' wallpaper, which is also said to have been designed by Maria Sèthe (Fig. 5). That project, a music room for his sister-in-law Irma Sèthe, a talented violinist, was carried out at the request of his mother-in-law, Louise Sèthe.[10] It is unclear whether or not Maria had a hand in designing the furniture for this room, but it is quite possible that in that period the couple worked together on interiors and furniture. In his memoirs, Van de Velde refers to early collaborations with Maria: 'Among the designs I made with Maria before our marriage was a detailed drawing of a chair and preliminary sketches for furniture for a small salon, which Emile van Mons, director of Beaux-Arts, had asked me to furnish.'[11] This passage suggests that Maria may have played a greater role at the design stage of the interior than is often acknowledged, given their joint creative work before their marriage. However, the extent to which Maria was involved in later interior designs is speculative, though the couple's close artistic collaboration in their early years clearly left its mark on Van de Velde's oeuvre.

Early on in their relationship, Maria Sèthe and Henry van de Velde also worked together in the field of textiles. Around 1893, they co-designed a curtain for a library.[12] Henry produced the definitive drawing and Maria carefully executed it in needlework.[13] In this way, Maria adopted the position of loyal assistant, responsible for implementing her husband's designs. Throughout her life, she

10 Maria Sèthe in the kitchen at Bloemenwerf, photographed by Emile Tassel and Charles Lefébure, c. 1900, KBR depot at AML, Brussels, FSIO 00882/0001/002/14.

11 Maria Sèthe and Henry van de Velde in the atelier on the first floor at Bloemenwerf, photographed by Emile Tassel and Charles Lefébure, c. 1900, KBR depot at AML, Brussels, FSIO 00882/0001/002/10.

provided that supportive role, assisting him with word and deed, including the quality control of his work. In 1895, she supervised the layout of the article 'Une prédication d'art' for *La Société Nouvelle* and executed the woodcuts after Henry's drawings for *Van Nu en Straks*. She also coordinated the transportation of furniture and other items Van de Velde was exhibiting in Siegfried Bing's gallery L'Art Nouveau in Paris in 1895.[14]

VILLA BLOEMENWERF: THE VAN DE VELDES'S GESAMTKUNSTWERK

In 1896, Henry van de Velde published an optimistic text in the Belgian Labour Party journal, *L'Avenir Social*, about the revival of industrial and decorative art.[15] This optimism stemmed from the success of Villa Bloemenwerf, the new home he had designed putting into practice his artistic theories. Named after a country house Henry and Maria had admired on their honeymoon in the Netherlands, Villa Bloemenwerf was a total concept that brought together all the art forms to create a harmonious and aesthetic home environment.[16] Van de Velde drew inspiration from William Morris and his Red House, and saw his own house as the ideal space for aesthetic development. He emphasised that work and private life should spill over into each other, which made the dwelling a place of creativity and joy. Villa Bloemenwerf became a meeting place for artists, writers and intellectuals, including Théo Van Rysselberghe, Henri de Toulouse-Lautrec, Johan Thorn Prikker and Emile Verhaeren.[17] Despite its success, in 1900 Henry and Maria left the house for a new phase in their lives in Germany, where Van de Velde's career would continue to flourish.

As well as planning the Villa Bloemenwerf building, Henry van de Velde also designed its furniture and wallpaper. In a bid to avoid partitions wherever possible, pretty well all the spaces, both living and work areas, were connected. One and the same principle determined not only the design of the house but also of the smallest utility object. The basic philosophy to which every element had to contribute was sobriety. The dining room Henry van de Velde created for Villa Bloemenwerf can be seen as a typical example of the concept underlying the design of most of his furniture. Fundamental principles were an impressively pure line and the tailoring of form to function. The design of the furniture gave rise to the basic principle that would define all Van de Velde's objects: line. Henry van de Velde was also clear in his opinion on ornamentation in furniture: 'I believe […] that the noblest ornament will always be abstract.'

14 Théo Van Rysselberghe, *Maria Sèthe at the Harmonium*, oil on canvas, 1891, KMSKA, Antwerp, 2690.
15 Henry van de Velde, armchair, 'Bloemenwerf' model, 1895-1896, Design Museum Gent.

12 & 13 Maria Sèthe in the central hall at Bloemenwerf in a tea gown designed by Henry van de Velde, c. 1896, photographed by Emile Tassel and Charles Lefébure, c.1900, KBR depot at AML, Brussels. The photograph was published in *Album moderner, nach Künstler-Entwürfen ausgeführter Damenkleider*, Düsseldorf, 1900, plate 4 (front) and plate 5 (back), Kunstmuseen Krefeld.

Furthermore, non-figurative ornament, the decoration, should always be subordinate to the piece of furniture itself. Indeed, Van de Velde saw ornamentation as a source of mediocrity and he used it sparingly.[18]

Maria played an essential role in the quality control and furnishing of the house. She chose the colours for various elements, including the front door and bathroom, and oversaw the finish of the interior. She picked out fabrics and dealt with the cabinet-making workshops that produced the furniture Henry had designed.[19]

As is well documented, Villa Bloemenwerf reflected their joint vision of a simple but refined lifestyle. Around 1900, Charles Lefébure, Ernest Solvay's private secretary, and Emile Tassel, engineer and professor at the Université Libre de Bruxelles, both amateur photographers, captured life at Villa Bloemenwerf in a series of photographs. Although staged, the pictures show its occupants' objective: a harmonious home, inspired by the English cottage style, where living and working meet.

Henry and Maria are both seen posing in a number of photographs. She is invariably wearing a dress designed for her by Henry with her input. The idea of designing clothing had stemmed from the total concept that Villa Bloemenwerf represented. According to Van de Velde, the presence of a lady dressed in haute couture in a setting like Villa Bloemenwerf would be sacrilegious.[20] Maria, who had made some of her own clothes before her marriage, helped him execute the designs, which began to appear around 1896. For example, a photograph taken in the atelier at Villa Bloemenwerf shows her working on a line of embroidery for a dress (Fig. 9).[21] In his memoirs, Van de Velde wrote: 'Applying the principles of rational conception to ladies' clothing was part of my aim to give the creation of objects for daily use a new starting point [...].'[22] Some of the clothing designs were probably intended for Maria's pregnancies. She bore seven children between 1895 and 1904 and so for a long period wore comfortable, loose dresses without a corset. Based on the idea that 'the dress is dictated by where it is to be worn', a view Van de Velde expounded in his 1902 article 'Das neue Kunst-Prinzip in der modernen Frauen-Kleidung' ('The new art principle in modern women's clothing'),[23] Maria's wardrobe included garden dresses, reception dresses for receiving guests at home, walking costumes (Fig. 7) for outdoors and evening gowns (Fig. 8). Most of the house dresses were made in softly draping velvet embellished with embroidery on the cuffs, the edge of the skirt, the chest and shoulders (Figs. 16-18). He advocated the 'accentuation of the visible seams'[24] and abstract ornamentation that 'emphasises the constructive cut of the dress' rather than the outmoded naturalistic adornments that serve no purpose.[25] This discourse is clearly an extension of his view of furniture design and is visualised in the Villa Bloemenwerf photographs. The line of the embroidery is in tune with the interior of the home, and the photographs of Maria posing next to the furniture emphasise this visual unity (Figs. 12 & 13).

Though Maria was Van de Velde's loyal assistant and remained at his side throughout her life, the spotlight was never on her, with one exception. At the *Sonderausstellung moderner nach Künstlerentwürfen ausgeführter Damenkleider* (Special Exhibition of Modern Ladies' Clothes based on Artists' Designs), held in Krefeld in Germany in 1900, Van de Velde showed a number of the designs he had produced with Maria. An album published to tie in with the exhibition contained thirty-two photographic reproductions of the dresses on show and lithographs of the embroidery details. We learn from the introduction, signed Maria van

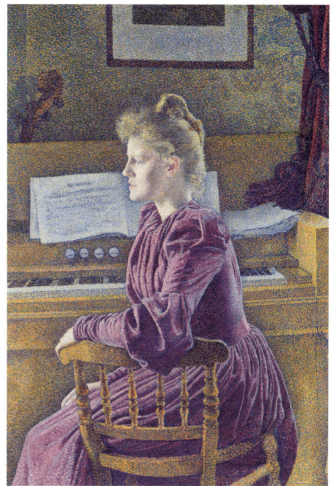

14

de Velde, that she too had a very clear view of the concept behind what was dubbed 'dress reform', which opposed the fashion concept she so condemned: '[...] "Fashion" is the great aberration, a major culprit in what the century amassed in the way of ugliness. It was dominated by whims and chance, and its creations bore their inevitable traces; the best it managed to produce were things of "good taste, decorous things, chic things". But it never achieved anything "beautiful" [...].'[26] Besides articulating her view on this subject in the introduction, she modelled most of the dresses designed by her husband. Photographs of these sessions appeared in the album, and Villa Bloemenwerf was the preferred setting.[27]

The photographs taken at Villa Bloemenwerf verify this largely neglected collaboration between Henry van de Velde and his invaluable partner Maria Sèthe. Later on in his memoirs, he stressed this in the passage about the memories awakened in him by the death of Maria in 1943: 'Fifty years in which she gave me all her devotion, all her thoughts, all her strength, accepting all the sacrifices, all the vicissitudes necessitated by my role and my mission.'[28]

15

Endnotes

1 ⎯⎯⎯ Henry van de Velde, *Récit de ma vie : Anvers-Bruxelles-Paris-Berlin. I 1863-1900*. eds. Anne Van Loo and Fabrice Van de Kerckhove (Brussels, Versa-Flammarion, 1992), 177–178.
2 ⎯⎯⎯ Van de Velde, *Récit 1863-1900*, 205–206.
3 ⎯⎯⎯ Perhaps thanks to her lessons with Georges Lemmen, a post-impressionist artist who ventured into applied-arts design around the same time as Van de Velde. See also Benjamin Zurstrassen, 'Behangselpapier van het echtpaar Van de Velde: Een quatre-mains?' in *Erfgoed Brussel, Dossier Art nouveau* 22 (2017): 57.
4 ⎯⎯⎯ Van de Velde, *Récit 1863-1900*, 211, note 4.
5 ⎯⎯⎯ Birgit Schulte, '"Ik ben de vrouw, die tot elke prijs uw geluk wil…": Maria Sèthe en Henry van de Velde – een biografische studie,' in *Henry van de Velde: Een Europees kunstenaar in zijn tijd*, eds. Klaus-Jürgen Sembach and Birgit Schulte (Antwerp: Pandora, 1993), 99.
6 ⎯⎯⎯ Henry van de Velde, 'Déblaiement d'art,' *La Société nouvelle* 10, 112 (1894): 444–456.
7 ⎯⎯⎯ Zurstrassen, 'Behangselpapier van het echtpaar Van de Velde: Een quatre-mains?' 58.
8 ⎯⎯⎯ Van de Velde, *Récit 1863-1900*, 239.
9 ⎯⎯⎯ Schulte, 'Ik ben de vrouw,' 99. The author states that the 'Dahlia' drawing dates from July 1893, when Maria Sèthe was working in the London studio of painter and designer of interiors Frank Brangwyn, who had previously been employed in the William Morris workshops. The drawing is said to have been the inspiration for Henry van de Velde's 'Dahlia' wallpaper.
10 ⎯⎯⎯ Van de Velde, *Récit 1863-1900*, 237. In his memoirs, however, Van de Velde mistakenly referred to the wallpaper used in this space as the 'Dahlia' wallpaper (Van de Velde, 287). The photograph of the interior shows the walls adorned with the 'Tulipes' wallpaper. For the photographs, see 'Henry van de Velde,' *L'Art décoratif* 1, 1 (1898): 20.
11 ⎯⎯⎯ Van de Velde, *Récit 1863-1900*, 237: 'Parmi les travaux que j'avais réalisés avec Maria avant notre mariage figurait aussi le dessin détaillé d'une chaise et des premières esquisses pour l'ameublement d'un petit salon que m'avait prié d'installer le directeur des Beaux-Arts, Emile van Mons […].'
12 ⎯⎯⎯ Antje Neumann, 'Decorative fabrics and applied textiles,' in *Henry van de Velde. Interior Design and Decorative Arts. Band II: Textiles*, eds. Thomas Föhl and Antje Neumann (Leipzig: Klassik Stiftung, 2014), 121.
13 ⎯⎯⎯ Schulte, 'Ik ben de vrouw,' 100.
14 ⎯⎯⎯ Schulte, 100–101.
15 ⎯⎯⎯ Henry van de Velde, 'Les Arts d'industrie et d'ornementation populaires,' *L'Avenir Social* 1, 3 (1896): 47–49; Henry van de Velde, 'Les Arts d'industrie et d'ornementation populaires,' *L'Avenir Social* 1, 4 (1896): 98–100; Henry van de Velde, 'Les Arts d'industrie et d'ornementation populaires,' *L'Avenir Social* 1, 8 (1896): 286–290.
16 ⎯⎯⎯ Van de Velde, *Récit 1863-1900*, 281.
17 ⎯⎯⎯ Van de Velde, 313.
18 ⎯⎯⎯ Werner Adriaenssens, 'Meubels, Interieurs. Het bewogen parcours,' in Thomas Föhl, Sabine Walter, Werner Adriaenssens, *Henry van de Velde. Passie, functie, schoonheid* (Tielt: Lannoo, 2013), 95–96. For the quote in this passage, see Henry van de Velde, 'Ein Kapitel über Entwurf und Bau moderner Möbel,' *Pan* 3, IV (1897-1898): 262: 'Ich glaube übrigens, dass der edelste Inhalt jeder Ornamentik immer das Abstrakte sein wird […].'
19 ⎯⎯⎯ Schulte, 'Ik ben de vrouw,' 101.
20 ⎯⎯⎯ Van de Velde, *Récit 1863-1900*, 375.
21 ⎯⎯⎯ Koninklijke Bibliotheek van België. Archives et Musée de la Littérature, Fonds Henry van de Velde.
22 ⎯⎯⎯ Van de Velde, *Récit 1863-1900*, 375: 'L'application des principes de la conception rationnelle à la toilette rentrait dans le cadre de l'action que je menais pour donner à la création d'objets d'usage quotidien un nouveau point de départ, valable pour l'ensemble de cette production.'
23 ⎯⎯⎯ Henry van de Velde, 'Das neue Kunst-Prinzip in der modernen Frauen-kleidung,' *Deutsche Kunst und Dekoration*, 10 (1902): 367: 'Die Toilette wird durch den Ort, wo man sie trägt, bestimmt […].'
24 ⎯⎯⎯ Henry van de Velde, *Die künstlerische Hebung der Frauentracht. Vortrag von Henry van de Velde* (Krefeld: Kramer & Baum, 1900), 24: 'Von den sichtbaren Nähten erwarte ich die Aufrichtigkeit in der Betonung dieser Ausführungsmittel und die Tendenz, dieselbe Aufrichtigkeit auf alle angewandten Mittel zu übertragen.'
25 ⎯⎯⎯ Van de Velde, *Die künstlerische Hebung der Frauentracht*, 25–26: 'In der Ornamentik, die ich begründet habe, und deren Berechtigung ich verteidige, sind die anzuwendenden Elemente Sache des Verstandes, der logischen Notwendigkeit. Wo der Künstler des Naturalismus ein Tier, eine Blume oder eine nackte Figur je nach seiner persönlichen Neigung und den augenblicklichen Eingebungen seiner Phantasie anbringt, füge ich eine Verzierung hinein, für die mir keine andere Wahl bleibt Sie wird genau der vorhandenen Raumform angepasst und ihre Motive entwickeln sich der Linienführung des Raumes entsprechend.'
26 ⎯⎯⎯ *Album de Robes de Dames exécutées d'après des projets d'artistes modernes figurant à l'exposition générale du vêtement Crefeld 1900 : avec préface de Madame Maria van de Velde* (Düsseldorf: Friedr. Wolfrum, s.d. [1900]), s.p.: '[…] "la Mode" est la grande aberrée, une grande coupable de ce que le siècle a amassé de laideurs. Le caprice et le hasard la régissant, ses créations portèrent les marques inévitables du caprice et du hasard ; et ce qu'elle put donner de mieux fut tout au plus, choses de "bon goût, choses de bon ton, choses de chic". Jamais elle n'atteignit à la chose "belle"; […].'
27 ⎯⎯⎯ *Album de Robes de Dames*, s.p.
28 ⎯⎯⎯ Henry van de Velde, *Récit de ma vie: Berne – Uttwil – La Haye – Otterlo – Bruxelles – Paris – New York – Oberägeri. 1917-1957 I*, compiled and annotated by Anne Van Loo with the assistance of Fabrice Van de Kerckhove (Brussels: Brepols-Versa, 2023), 560: 'Cinquante années durant lesquelles elle m'avait voué tout son attachement, toutes ses pensées, toutes ses forces; durant lesquelles elle avait accepté tous les sacrifices, toutes les vicissitudes qui comportait l'accomplissement de mon rôle et de ma mission.'

16 Henry van de Velde, Cornély embroidered cuffs from a velvet tea gown, c. 1896, Museum für Gestaltung Zürich, Decorative Arts Collection, ZHdK.
17 Henry van de Velde, Cornély embroidered collar from a velvet tea gown, c. 1896, Museum für Gestaltung Zürich, Decorative Arts Collection, ZHdK.
18 Henry van de Velde, Cornély embroidered skirt border from a velvet tea gown, c. 1896, Museum für Gestaltung Zürich, Decorative Arts Collection, ZHdK.
19 Henry van de Velde, embroidery design for a tea gown, 1896, Kunstmuseen Krefeld.

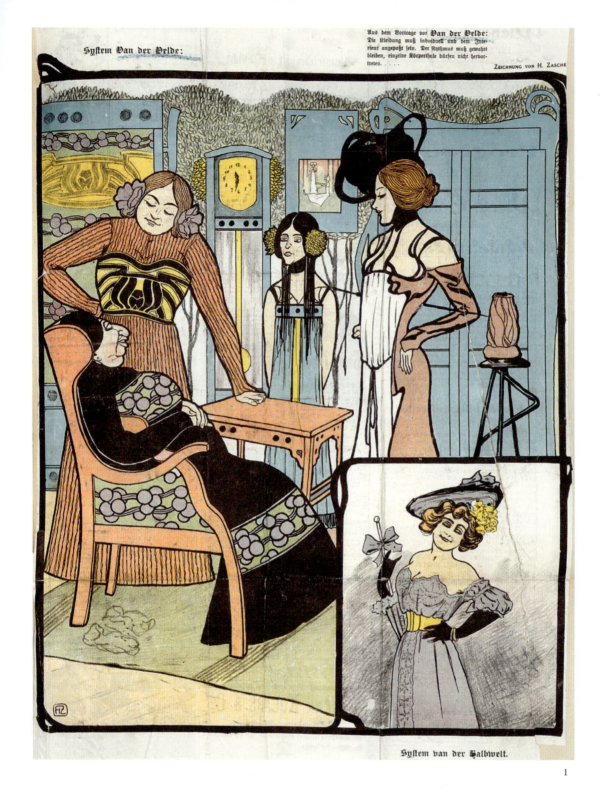

1 Theodor Zasche, 'System van de Velde', *Neues Wiener Witzblatt*, 30 March 1901, Kunstmuseen Krefeld.
Text on the print: 'From the lecture by Van de Velde: clothing must be individual and adapted to the interior. Rhythm must be preserved, individual body parts should not stand out...'

THE 'ELEVATION OF WOMEN'S DRESS' AROUND 1900: WOMEN AND THEIR CLOTHES BETWEEN DECORATION AND EMANCIPATION[1]

Magdalena Holzhey

Germany's first-ever exhibition of artistic reform dresses opened in August 1900 in Krefeld – one of the most important centres of the European silk industry at that time. While women's dress reform had been on the agenda and widely discussed for several years, it was the *Sonder-Ausstellung moderner Damen-Kostüme nach Künstler-Entwürfen* (Special Exhibition of Modern Ladies' Costumes Based on Artist Designs) that elevated the dress itself to a work of art. The exhibition's initiator was the director of Krefeld's Kaiser Wilhelm Museum, Friedrich Deneken, in collaboration with Henry van de Velde and the Hamburg-based painter Alfred Mohrbutter. A total of ten male and female artists took part in the exhibition. Most of the designs on show were by Henry van de Velde, whose dresses for the home, for going out into town and for social occasions (including the famous tea gowns) by and large followed the new principles that he wanted to see applied to womenswear in general: beauty, logic and an emphasis on the specific properties of the material.

The exhibition of 1900 was a stimulus in more ways than one. When Deneken took over as director of the Kaiser Wilhelm Museum in 1897, he did so with the explicit aim of intensifying collaboration between artists and local craftsmen. For the Krefeld silk weavers' Deuß & Oetker Seidenweberei, the artistic dress exhibition was a crucial factor in their decision to launch a line of 'artists' silks' patterned with designs by artists such as Van de Velde (Figs. 3, 4 & 9), Mohrbutter and others.[2] From an economic point of view, the business was not a success, and it was discontinued after a few years. Both Van de Velde's artistic dresses and silk designs attracted attention, particularly in artistic circles, and they were staged by personalities such as Elisabeth Förster-Nietzsche (Fig. 2) and Gertrud Osthaus.[3]

With the corset still dominating conventional fashion, some of the dresses on show in Krefeld still included a visible waistline, but the exhibition was still first and foremost perceived as a showcase for the dress-reform movement. Its success can be gauged from the unusually broad coverage it received in the press, which acknowledged and discussed the social and cultural ramifications of the undertaking.[4] It clearly showed how much clothing around 1900 conveyed gender relationships and, thus, reflected the basic structure of society. This also explains why the reform dress, which dispensed with the corset, was seen as a massive attack on the existing order. The discussion around new clothing styles for women was closely connected with the nascent emancipation movement. The involvement of women's associations for reform fashion was part of their claim to participation in political and social life, which included the artistic field. If a woman wished to be active as an artist around 1900, she not only had to struggle against the extreme prejudices which considered women physically and intellectually inferior, but she also faced stark limitations on educational opportunities.[5]

In the applied arts, the situation was different. Thanks to the renewal efforts in that field around the turn of the century, women already enjoyed broader career opportunities. Glasgow and Vienna in particular were pioneers in this respect, but German workshops in places such as Munich or Hellerau also offered women permanent positions. Most women, however, worked with textiles and made home designs because these were considered to be their most intrinsic fields. Traditionally, the interior

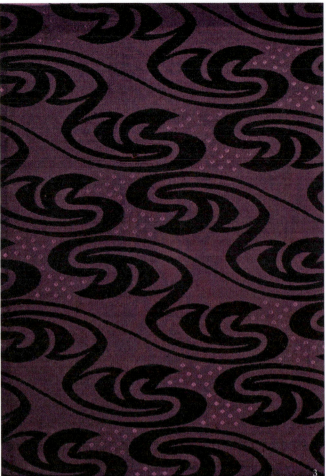

2 Elisabeth Förster-Nietzsche in a dress made of Henry van de Velde's fabric, photographed by Nicola Perscheid, 1903, Klassik-Stiftung Weimar.
3 Henry van de Velde, 'Künstlerseide' dress fabric, 1901, Kunstmuseen Krefeld, ZV 1982/395.
4 Henry van de Velde, 'Künstlerseide' dress fabric, 1901, Kunstmuseen Krefeld, ZV 1982/392 a, b.

5 Maria Sèthe in the central hall at Bloemenwerf in a house dress designed by Henry van de Velde, c. 1896, from *Album Robes de Dames*, 1900, plate 6, KMKG-MRAH, Brussels.

and textiles were associated with the feminine, a link that the sociocultural, anthropological and psychological writings of the late nineteenth century took to such an extreme that the German term *Frauenzimmer* was transferred from the occupied room ('women's room') to the person occupying it ('woman').[6]

The 'housewife' and the closed-off space of the domestic sphere are inventions of the bourgeois nineteenth century. They went hand in hand with a gender-specific ideology that kept them in a state of dependence and subservience. This was underscored by the pseudoscientific justification that women lack creativity and genius and are, therefore, particularly well suited to reproductive tasks.[7] At the same time, over the course of the nineteenth century, the private sphere evolved into an extended space of aesthetic orchestration. In the debates over historicism and necessary reforms, the applied arts in particular became a catalyst for establishing a new, modern style. Architecture became the covering of the interior, comparable to clothes being the shell covering the body: 'cladding' things was seen as analogous to dressing one's own body. This is the only possible explanation for the interest of Jugendstil architects in defining their new ideas first by way of the design of the house and its furniture, and then by transferring their formal language to the housewife's dress so that the woman's outward appearance reflected the spatial presentation.

The idea that only the male gender could represent modern culture was widespread around 1900. The differences between the sexes, which were supposedly based on natural laws, are also reflected in Henry van de Velde's writings on women's clothing, in which he largely denies women the ability to design the ornament that adorns reform clothing: 'Because not all women, even if they have taste, are able to invent suitable ornaments.'[8] The ornament of the new style remained a matter for men: it was rational, logical and beautiful; corresponded to both moral and aesthetic principles; and served to rationalise the excessively ornamental quality of historicism.

For the Van de Veldes, the salon became the place to present the new artistic dress.[9] Maria Sèthe, whom Henry van de Velde married in 1894, personified the role of the artist's wife in almost exemplary fashion. Sèthe, an artist herself, influenced her husband significantly and became his closest collaborator. The design of comfortable, artistically designed women's clothing here formed part of the aesthetic design of everyday life. Maria wrote not only the text for *Album moderner, nach Künstler-Entwürfen ausgeführter Damenkleider* ('Album of Modern Women's Dresses Designed by Artists'), published in 1900 for the exhibition in Krefeld, but also a report on the exhibition in the journal *Dekorative Kunst*.[10] She was also clearly decisively involved in the design of the clothes, as her preface in the album suggests.[11] Henry van de Velde presumably limited himself, in addition to the constructive emphasis on draping, to the design of the ornaments.

The ambiguity of the distribution of their roles is revealed in Maria's public appearances in artistic dresses which she had photographed over the years and published in the Krefeld *Album*. She was at once a model and an active housewife: her poses show her both performing everyday tasks intended to underscore the comfort of the new clothing and as an item of decoration within the overall Gesamtkunstwerk of the interior architecture of the house (Fig. 5). The latter is in keeping with the concept of the dress as a work of art, but it forces her as its wearer into a largely passive role, whereas with few exceptions, the man remains invisible but is named as the reformer of social changes which, in turn, concern women. In a 1911 essay on Van de Velde's new style, art critic Karl Scheffler stressed the atmospheric connection of interior space and the image of women: 'these interiors first come completely alive when decoratively dressed women move within them.'[12] Although it is clearly more powerfully anchored in real, everyday life, it is clearly still an idealised world being expressed here. As early as 1901, Gunta Beeg was criticising the artistic reform of fashion from the perspective of the emancipation movement in this spirit: the woman herself is said to be the work of art and the dress merely the frame; she is not a lifeless object whose surface could be decorated[13] – an observation that also inspired contemporaries to caricature (Fig. 1).

Endnotes

1 _____ This text is based on the essays published in Ina Ewers-Schultz and Magdalena Holzhey, *Tailored for Freedom. The Artistic Dress around 1900 in Fashion, Art and Society*, exh. cat. Kunstmuseen Krefeld (Munich: Hirmer, 2018).
2 _____ See Linda Tschöpe, 'Deuss & Oetker's Künstlerseide,' in *Textilien*, ed. Thomas Föhl and Antje Neumann, vol. 2 of *Henry van de Velde: Raumkunst und Kunsthandwerk, Werkverzeichnis in sechs Bänden* (Leipzig: Seemann, 2014), 26–31. Carl Lange's silk factory also produced 'artists' silks', including some after designs by Peter Behrens and Richard Riemerschmid.
3 _____ See Antje Neumann, '"The Fairies Have Strewn Flowers along the Way". The Textile Designer Henry van de Velde and his Weimar Circle,' in Ewers-Schultz and Holzhey 2018 (see footnote 1), 31–35, here 31.
4 _____ See also Gerda Breuer, 'Künstlerkleid und Eigenkleid: Zur "Sonderausstellung moderner Damenkostüme nach Künstlerentwürfen" in Krefeld 1900,' *Die Heimat* 57 (1986): 24–30.
5 _____ See Jutta Hülsewig-Johnen, 'Starke Frauen: Die Kunst ist weiblich,' in *Einfühlung und Abstraktion: Die Moderne der Frauen in Deutschland*, ed. Jutta Hülsewig-Johnen and Henrike Mund, exh. cat. Kunsthalle Bielefeld (Cologne: Wienand, 2015), 13–21.
6 _____ Irene Nierhaus, 'Text + Textil: Zur geschlechtlichen Strukturierung von Material in der Architektur von Innenräumen,' in *Um-Ordnung: Angewandte Künste und Geschlecht in der Moderne*, ed. Cordula Bischoff and Christina Threuter (Marburg: Jonas, 1999), 84–94, esp. 89.
7 _____ See Ulrike Döcker, Die Ordnung der bürgerlichen Welt: Verhaltensideale und soziale Praktiken im 19. Jahrhundert (Frankfurt am Main: Campus, 1994).
8 _____ 'Denn nicht alle Frauen, wenn sie auch Geschmack haben, sind imstande, geeignete Ornamente zu erfinden.' Henry van de Velde, *Die künstlerische Hebung der Frauentracht* (Krefeld: Kramer & Baum, 1900), 32.
9 _____ According to Gabriele Brandstätter, *Tanz-Lektüren: Körperbilder und Raumfiguren der Avantgarde* (Frankfurt am Main: Fischer, 1995), 119.
10 _____ Maria van de Velde, 'Sonderausstellung moderner Damenkostüme,' *Dekorative Kunst* 4 (1901): 41–47.
11 _____ Maria van de Velde, preface, in *Album moderner, nach Künstler-Entwürfen ausgeführter Damenkleider* (Düsseldorf: Wolfrum, [1900]).
12 _____ Karl Scheffler, 'Henry van de Velde und der neue Stil,' *Kunst und Künstler: Illustrierte Monatsschrift für bildende Kunst und Kunstgeschichte* 9 (1911): 119–33, esp. 129.
13 _____ G[unta] B[eeg], 'Zur künstlerischen Reform der Mode,' *Illustrierte Frauen-Zeitung* 28/21, no. 3 (November 1, 1901): 76.

6

7

6 Henry van de Velde, carpet for a bedroom at Villa Esche, 1908, Design Museum Gent, 1976-0245.
7 Henry van de Velde, lady's 'hairdressing chair' V No. 2, 1897, Design Museum Gent, FH-0083.
8 Shoulder trim decorated with chenille thread from the Maria Sèthe Bequest, c. 1898, Museum für Gestaltung Zürich, Decorative Arts Collection, ZHdK, KGS-1958-0080 a-b.
9 Henry van de Velde, 'Künstlerseide' dress fabric, 1901, Kunstmuseen Krefeld.

8

9

1 Josef Hoffmann, Palais Stoclet in Brussels, 1905-1911, MAK – Museum of Applied Arts, Vienna, LI 10875-1.
2 Interior of the Flöge sisters' fashion house designed by Josef Hoffmann and executed by the Wiener Werkstätte, 1904, from *Deutsche Kunst und Dekoration*, 16, 523, VIII Vol. 1904/05, June, No. 9, Heidelberg University.

LINKING FASHION WITH ARCHITECTURE AND INTERIOR DESIGN: THE WIENER WERKSTÄTTE, SCHWESTERN FLÖGE AND PAUL POIRET

Lara Steinhäußer

In 1903, architect Josef Hoffmann founded the design association Wiener Werkstätte with his colleague at the Vienna Kunstgewerbeschule, Koloman Moser, a graphic designer and painter. Their ambitious plans, inspired by the ideals of the British Arts and Crafts movement, were supported by visionary financier Fritz Waerndorfer, an heir to a wealthy textile-producing family. Hoffmann was the last of the original trio to remain with the Wiener Werkstätte until its dissolution in 1932, as Moser left in 1907 and Waerndorfer in 1914.[1] By the time the Wiener Werkstätte had to shut down, it had operated for almost three decades. Throughout its existence, the textile department, founded in 1910 and closely aligned with the fashion department that opened in early 1911, was the most financially successful branch.[2]

While contemporary architect and author of *Ornament and Crime* Adolf Loos advocated for the distinction between objects of art and utility,[3] painter Gustav Klimt and a group of like-minded artists including Hoffmann and Moser sought to promote the equality of art and craft, founding the Viennese Secession in 1897. Hoffmann and Moser were also part of the so-called 'Klimt-group', which left the Secession in 1905 along with the famous Viennese painter.

In that same year, the Wiener Werkstätte published its theoretical foundation known as the *Arbeitsprogramm*. This program outlined their primary goal of producing objects across various domains – from book bindings and jewellery to furniture – aiming to create a Gesamtkunstwerk of individual hand-made items that would counteract common machine and mass production. The manifesto-like work program also indicated that clothing design was included in the areas of daily life the Wiener Werkstätte intended to address.[4] However, looking at the Wiener Werkstätte's history reveals that they not only produced objects in their own workshops but also frequently commissioned other companies – such as Portois & Fix for furniture and Backhausen for textiles – to produce for them. Additionally, they distributed and sold products from external companies and artists in their shops, including ceramics by Wiener Keramik.

3   Emilie Flöge in her fashion house wearing a gown designed by Eduard Josef Wimmer-Wisgrill and made by the Flöge sisters. Photographed by Madame d'Ora, before 1910. Museum für Kunst und Gewerbe Hamburg, Madame d'Ora Bequest.

4   Emilie Flöge wearing a gown by Gustav Klimt and Wiener Werkstätte jewellery, *Deutsche Kunst und Dekoration*, 19, 1906-1907, 70. MAK – Museum of Applied Arts, Vienna, WWF 124-24-1.

5   Josef Hoffmann, cupboard made by the Wiener Werkstätte for the Flöge sisters' fashion house, 1904, private collection – Galerie Yves Macaux.

6

7

8

9

6 Josef Hoffmann and J. & L. Lobmeyr, carafe, wine glass and champagne coupe from the *Var B* series, 1912, Kunstmuseen Krefeld.
7 & 9 Josef Hoffmann, gown with squares and rosettes, c. 1910, MAK – Museum of Applied Arts, Vienna, WWF 169-15 and WWF 124-22-1.
8 Josef Hoffmann, lady's briefcase, gold-embossed black leather, c. 1910, German Textile Museum Krefeld, 23699.
10 Josef Hoffmann, white coat with black longitudinal seams, c. 1910, MAK – Museum of Applied Arts, Vienna, WWGP-418l.

11

12

11 Koloman Moser, armchair for Purkersdorf Sanatorium, 1903, Leopold Museum, Vienna, 4354.
12 Wiener Werkstätte, glass mosaic for the Flöge sisters' fashion house, 1904, MAK – Museum of Applied Arts, Vienna, GL 2834.

FASHION FROM THE 'KLIMT-GROUP' – GUSTAV KLIMT, SCHWESTERN FLÖGE AND THE WIENER WERKSTÄTTE'S ARTISTIC FASHION

In 1905 the Wiener Werkstätte began collaborating with Gustav Klimt on the Palais Stoclet in Brussels (Fig. 1) for the Belgian engineer Adolphe Stoclet, who had met Hoffmann while working in Vienna. There exists a myth suggesting that the Wiener Werkstätte only started producing women's dresses after Madame Stoclet was seen in the Gesamtkunstwerk Palais Stoclet wearing a mismatching gown by Paul Poiret.[5] Although a 1911 article quoting Fritz Waerndorfer mentioned that the Wiener Werkstätte had indeed designed dresses and accessories for Madame Stoclet,[6] it is not known whether the myth's claimed sighting really served as the impetus for the founding of the Wiener Werkstätte's fashion department.

It is plausible that prior to the official opening of the fashion department, Hoffmann and Moser[7] had already designed costumes and dresses for select Wiener Werkstätte clients, as suggested by Adolf Loos's recommendation for Hoffmann to establish a women's fashion department,[8] as well as a satirical play by Fritz Waerndorfer from 1909 depicting an average day in the Wiener Werkstätte.[9] While around 1910 the Wiener Werkstätte started producing fashion, in the preceding years their artistic clothing designs were likely rather similar to the anti-fashion ideas of the *Reformkleid* which Henry van de Velde had already propagated around 1900. In 1906, a special issue of *Deutsche Kunst und Dekoration* dedicated to the Wiener Werkstätte featured corsetless dresses in the *Reformkleid* style which, according to the description, had been designed and photographed by Klimt and executed by 'Schwestern Pfluege' (!) (Fig. 4). The dresses were worn by Emilie Flöge, who was the creative director of the company Schwestern Flöge, which she ran with her two sisters. Although many believe Klimt only took the photographs, there is correspondence between Waerndorfer and Hermann Muthesius, who was supposed to write an article on the Wiener Werkstätte for *Deutsche Kunst und Dekoration,* which confirms Klimt also had a hand in the design of the clothes.[10]

Emilie Flöge played a significant role in the artistic-dress scene in Vienna at that time, especially in her connections with Klimt and the Wiener Werkstätte. She not only modelled for Klimt, who worked closely with the Wiener Werkstätte for the Palais Stoclet[11] and the Cabaret Fledermaus, but also served as a mannequin for the Wiener Werkstätte. Her boutique also produced dresses for them (Fig. 3). The Schwestern Flöge's salon in the so-called Casa Piccola on Vienna's Mariahilferstraße (Fig. 2), designed by Hoffmann and Moser in 1904, also sold jewellery by the Wiener Werkstätte, which Emilie herself wore as well.[12] Flöge is particularly known for the distinctive wide and often striped dresses and caftans which she was frequently seen wearing in pictures with Klimt around 1908 and 1909 (Fig. 14).

These garments reflect the aesthetic of Koloman Moser, who is said to have designed similar ornamented clothes for his wife Ditha and most likely for the opera singer Anna Bahr-Mildenburg and her husband, writer Hermann Bahr.[13] A later Poiret dress from his wife's estate (Fig. 16) was likely produced under the influence of the Viennese artists who were internationally renowned for their black-and-white designs. Especially the dress's cut echoes documented designs by Josef Hoffmann (Fig. 18) showcasing the Empire waistline trend as well as the influence of Indian dresses that were worn by women in Vienna's artistic circles at the beginning of the twentieth century.[14]

13 Gustav Klimt, portrait of Emilie Flöge, 1902, Wien Museum.
14 Emilie Flöge in Schörfling am Attersee, photographed by Heinrich Böhler, c. 1909.
15 Emilie Flöge, photographed by Madame d'Ora, c. 1909, Museum für Kunst und Gewerbe Hamburg, Madame d'Ora Bequest, P1965.420.22.

16 Paul Poiret, linen house dress with tobacco-coloured stripes, made up of panels, c. 1920, from the Denise Poiret Bequest, Fondation Azzedine Alaïa, Paris.
17 Maria Grazia Chiuri and Pierpaolo Piccioli for Valentino, coat with graphic motifs, Autumn-Winter 2015-2016, photographed by Dan Jackson for *WSJ. Magazine*, August 2015.

18 Josef Hoffmann, silk dress with appliqués, made for a fancy dress ball, c. 1910, MAK - Museum of Applied Arts, Vienna, T 11827.

19

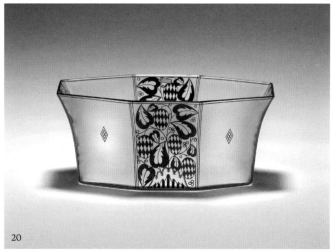

20

21

19   Josef Hoffmann for J. & L. Lobmeyr, glass flacon with leaf decoration, 1913, MAK – Museum of Applied Arts, Vienna, WI 1632-1.
20   Josef Hoffmann for J. & L. Lobmeyr, glass jardinière with leaf decoration, 1913, MAK – Museum of Applied Arts, Vienna, WI 1674.
21   Josef Hoffmann for J. & L. Lobmeyr, glass comb tray with leaf decoration, 1913, MAK – Museum of Applied Arts, Vienna, WI 1632-2.

22 Josef Hoffmann, machine-knotted wool carpet for Palais Stoclet, 'Bellflower' model, 1910, Leopold Museum, Vienna, 6117.

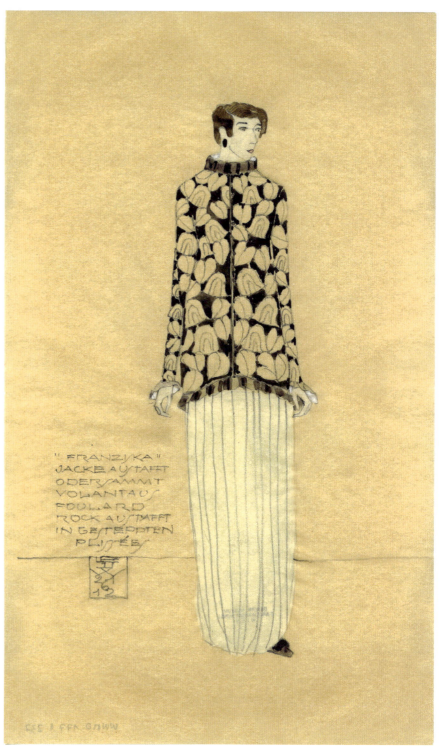

23 Eduard Josef Wimmer-Wisgrill, design sketch for the 'Franziska' jacket in the 'Jagdfalke' fabric, designed by Josef Hoffmann, 1912, MAK – Museum of Applied Arts, Vienna, WWMO 183-2.
24 Josef Hoffmann, book cover in 'Jagdfalke' fabric, made by the Wiener Werkstätte, 1915, MAK – Museum of Applied Arts, Vienna, T10511.

25 Interior of the Flöge sisters' apartment with 'Heimchen' curtains and wallpaper, c. 1911, MAK – Museum of Applied Arts, Vienna, WWF 236-1.

The comparison of an armchair (Fig. 11) designed by Moser with the clothing described above reveals a shared approach to decorative surface treatment in both clothing and furniture. Also, Hoffmann's cupboard design for Schwestern Flöge (Fig. 5) mirrors the architectural principles of the Wiener Werkstätte (Figs. 1 & 2), emphasizing a cohesive aesthetic across different fields. A coat design by Hoffmann from about 1910[15] (Fig. 10), again with dark outlines accentuating the verticality, shows how this equality of surfaces is typical for the Wiener Werkstätte's Gesamtkunstwerk approach.

Additionally, it was common at the Wiener Werkstätte for wallpapers and textiles produced after 1910 to feature the same patterns[16]. A textile design available at the Wiener Werkstätte by architect Eduard Josef Wimmer-Wisgrill (Fig. 26), who also designed the interior of Flöge's private apartment with Biedermeier elements in about 1911, shows he not only used it there for both walls and furniture[17] (Fig. 25) but also for a costume design (Fig. 28). When the Wiener Werkstätte fashion department was opened in 1911, it was under the direction of Wimmer-Wisgrill, who was often referred to as the 'Poiret of Vienna'.

Another interesting episode from the history of the Wiener Werkstätte perfectly illustrates the proximity of fashion and interior design as a part of an overall aesthetic or a lifestyle concept at that time. It prominently features the renowned French couturier Poiret.

'GERMAN' FASHION AND INTERIOR DESIGN MADE IN PARIS AND VIENNA: THE CREATIVE LIAISON BETWEEN PAUL POIRET AND THE WIENER WERKSTÄTTE

In November 1911 Paul Poiret visited Vienna during his great tour through Central and Eastern Europe, which included cities such as Moscow, St. Petersburg, Warsaw, Bucharest, Budapest and Berlin.

The collection of the MAK Vienna holds a poster for '*Paul Poiret in Vienna*' (Fig. 30) advertising an event held on three consecutive afternoons from 27 to 29 November at the Viennese education centre Urania. The poster announced that the event's proceeds would be donated to charitable causes. The program included a cinematographic presentation, a lecture by Poiret on his creations, and a live fashion show featuring clothing presented on

26 Eduard Josef Wimmer-Wisgrill for the Wiener Werkstätte, 'Heimchen' fabric, c.1911, MAK – Museum of Applied Arts, Vienna, T 11379-2-1.

mannequins.[18] According to Austrian press reports, the poster had been designed by Josef Hoffmann, who also took care of the artistic setting of the fashion presentations.[19]

The motif for the poster was taken from the album *Les Choses de Paul Poiret vues par Georges Lepape* that Lepape had created for Poiret in 1911. This indicated that Hoffmann's contributions were primarily focused on the writings and the layout of the poster, which was printed by the local Viennese company Gebrüder Rosenbaum. Additionally, Lepape's graphic work was exhibited in Vienna alongside sculptures from the artists' association Mánes from Prague during Poiret's 'dress rehearsal' at the premises of the artists' group Hagenbund on 26 November. It is noteworthy that this premiering event featured models parading among the visitors, but there was insufficient space for a lecture in this case. Photographs from one of Poiret's fashion shows at the venue Urania (Fig. 29) reveal that Hoffmann's artistic setting there incorporated Wiener Werkstätte textiles, including 'Ameise', 'Kohleule' and 'Krametsvogel' for cushions, arranged on a chaise longue reminiscent of the Empire period. A ceramic statue by Michael Powolny, available for sale at the Wiener Werkstätte's store, was also part of the artistic arrangement.

Numerous articles in Austrian newspapers reported on the visit of the 'Parisian fashion king' to their capital city. While there are many reports suggesting that the Viennese tailors were concerned about competition from Poiret, the *Neue Freie Presse* focused on his connections with the Wiener Werkstätte.[20] Its article mentioned that Poiret's wife Denise wore a dress made from a fabric by Eduard Josef Wimmer-Wisgrill and that Poiret had already been a customer of the Wiener Werkstätte for some time. Additionally, it stated that Poiret aimed to reform the decorative arts in Paris and had asked the leading artists of the Wiener Werkstätte to 'see in him ... their most enthusiastic apostle for Paris'. The article further indicated that Poiret planned to build a new villa designed by 'Professor Hoffmann' and also intended to incorporate Wiener Werkstätte products into the assortment of his existing palace, which is why 'major agreements were concluded between Poiret and the Wiener Werkstätte for this purpose'. Other newspapers reported that Poiret

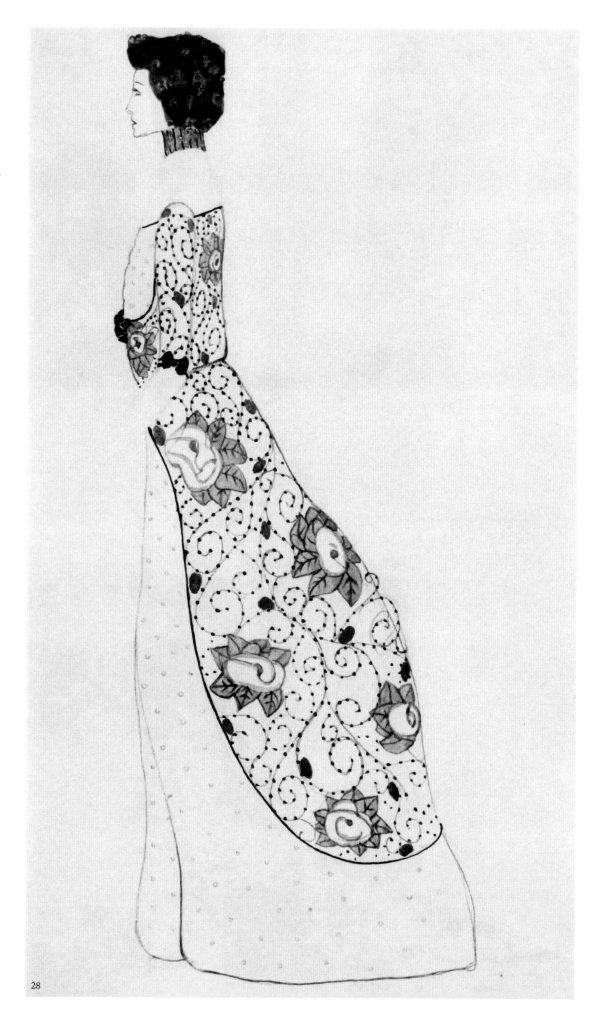

27 Martin Margiela, dress from the Wiener Werkstätte-inspired *Les Orientalistes* collection, Spring-Summer 1985, photographed by Patrick Robyn.
28 Eduard Josef Wimmer-Wisgrill, design sketch for a dress with 'Heimchen' motif, 1912, from *Jahrbuch Deutschen Werkbundes* 1912, 89.

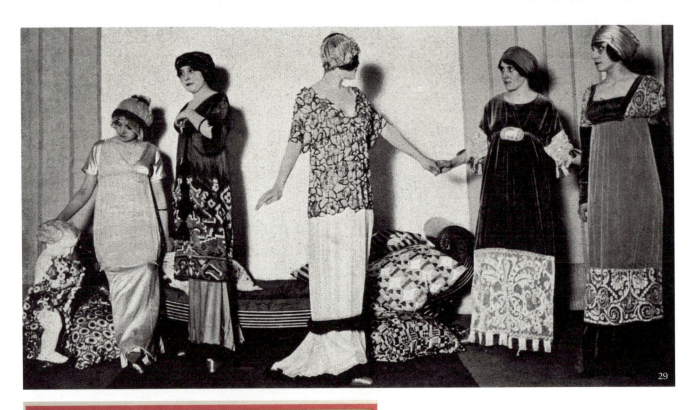

29 Mannequins at Poiret's fashion show at the Urania in Vienna in 1911, from *Světozor*, Vol. 12, No. 15, 7 December 1911, 356, National Library of the Czech Republic, Prague.

30 Poster 'Paul Poiret in Vienna', with a drawing by Georges Lepape, 1911, MAK – Museum of Applied Arts, Vienna, PI 1748.

purchased a dress designed by Hoffmann as a model for his own work.[21] While the veracity of all these detailed claims is uncertain, the press coverage affirms that collaborations were intended and reflects mutual inspiration between Poiret and the Viennese designers.

The rediscovery of Hoffmann's plans for Poiret's villa on glass-plate negatives in the MAK's Wiener Werkstätte archive (Fig. 31) in 2021 has shed light on a significant architectural project that was never carried out.[22] Austrian journalist and salonniére Berta Zuckerkandl-Szeps had previously documented these plans in her 1923 article 'Paul Poiret and the Klimt group' for the *Neues Wiener Journal* when Poiret visited Vienna during another fashion tour. According to her description, Hoffmann's design for Poiret's palace 'on the current Avenue Viktor Emanuel' is 'still one of the most beautiful [...] created by the great architect Josef Hoffmann (who was so little utilised by Austrians). A small theatre was built into the house, whose galleries led to the reception rooms.'[23] Tensions between Hoffmann and Waerndorfer stemming from the steep invoices Waerndorfer sent to Poiret ultimately led to Hoffmann's decision to distance his architecture office from the Wiener Werkstätte.[24]

In her memoirs, Zuckerkandl recounted arranging a meeting between Klimt, Hoffmann and Poiret, a claim confirmed in Poiret's autobiography.[25] After Poiret's 1911 visit to the Austrian pavilion designed by Hoffmann for the *Esposizione Internazionale* in Rome, the meeting came about through Zuckerkandl's sister Sophie, who was married to the brother of French statesman Georges Clemenceau and was a customer of Poiret.[26] In her memoirs, Zuckerkandl additionally highlighted a dress by Paul Poiret, named *Valse de Vienne*, which debuted in 1912 at one of his fashion shows in Paris and was made from Wiener Werkstätte fabric and passementerie from the Viennese Kunstgewerbeschule.[27]

It is well known that Poiret utilised fabrics from the Wiener Werkstätte in his designs, particularly in the 1920s.[28] Notably, he incorporated fabrics designed by Dagobert Peche, who began working for the Wiener Werkstätte around 1911 or 1912. Two specific patterns that Poiret used are the 'Rainbow' fabric, which he used for lining a coat (Figs. 32 & 33), and the 'Diomedes' fabric, which was not only used for a lining but also for a dress.

Peche's scholarship to Paris in 1912 likely facilitated his interaction with Poiret, who had just recently made his purchases from the Wiener Werkstätte and maintained connections with Hoffmann regarding his villa. Some of Peche's floral designs for textiles, which are reminiscent of the woodcut technique, share stylistic similarities with fabrics created by Raoul Dufy for Poiret and Bianchini-Férier.[29]

The Musèe des Arts Décoratifs in Paris has a collection of drawings by graphic artist and costume and textile designer Victor Lhuer that includes some designs for garments by Poiret from the early 1910s. One of these designs features an attached Wiener Werkstätte fabric sample, namely Mizzi Vogl's 'Kanarienvogel', indicating it was intended to be used in the dress's design.[30] Lhuer also developed a graphic pattern for French magazine *Femina* in 1914 that was based on Josef Hoffmann's *Kohleule*, which had been among the textiles used in Poiret's fashion shows in Vienna.[31]

As Heather Hess[32] and Angela Völker[33] have demonstrated elsewhere, some of Poiret's textile designs were most likely based on Wiener Werkstätte designs, but Guy-Pierre Fauconnet made some sketches for furniture for Poiret's design enterprise Martine (Figs. 37 & 38) that reveal striking similarities to Wiener Werkstätte chairs after Hoffmann's design (Figs. 35 & 36).

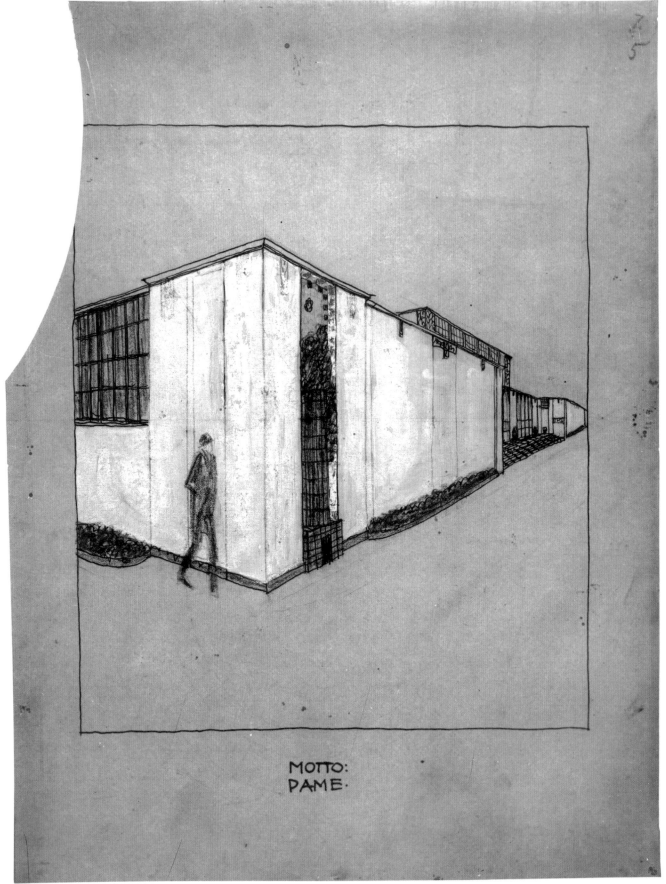

To this day, the literature has always emphasised that while the Wiener Werkstätte was influenced by Poiret's fashion, the French couturier himself was inspired by Viennese ideas for his design company Martine, named after one of his daughters, which opened in 1912. Poiret himself denied his closeness to the Wiener Werkstätte designers in his 1930 autobiography, even though the similarities and connections had been frequently reported on in German-speaking and American media.[34] This denial was most likely caused by his French contemporaries' interpretation of his stylistic closeness to the Wiener Werkstätte as collaboration with the 'German' enemy, especially after the outbreak of the First World War.[35] Although there is ample proof of the influence of the Wiener Werkstätte's designs, the informal management of the École Martine allowing girls to work experimentally seems rather to have been modelled after Franz Cižek's art class for children at the Viennese Kunstgewerbeschule, where young students were taught to express themselves freely.[36] Also, as Poiret stressed in his autobiography, unlike the Wiener Werkstätte, he was not the biggest fan of the idea of the Gesamtkunstwerk, nor was stylistic cohesion among his primary concerns for Atelier Martine.

However, the cross-connections between French fashion and Viennese interior design can be traced back to the late 1920s: not only is the Austrian architect and director of the Wiener Werkstätte shop in New York, Joseph Urban, said to have designed costumes for Poiret in the 1920s,[37] but in 1929 former Wiener Werkstätte artist and ceramics specialist Vally Wieselthier joined forces with the German designers Bruno Paul and Lucian Bernhard as well as Paul Poiret to establish the Contempora design collective in New York.[38]

It is still fascinating today to trace these collaborations. They illustrate the intersections between (French) fashion and (Viennese) interior design during that period which demonstrate how the theoretical connections between architecture and textile that Gottfried Semper with his *Bekleidungsprinzip* had already established in 1864 were a fertile breeding ground for modern design in the early twentieth century.

31   Josef Hoffmann, design sketch for a villa for Paul Poiret, 1912, MAK – Museum of Applied Arts, Vienna, WWGP 1998.

32 & 33 Paul Poiret, 'Maroc' wool coat lined with 'Diomedes' Wiener Werkstätte fabric, c. 1923, Fondation Azzedine Alaïa, Paris.
34 Dagobert Peche, 'Diomedes' fabric sample, 1919, MAK - Museum of Applied Arts, Vienna, WWS 157.

Endnotes

1 _____ For more details on the history of the Wiener Werkstätte, see e.g. Peter Noever, ed., *Yearning for Beauty: The Wiener Werkstätte and the Stoclet House* (Berlin: Hatje Cantz, 2006) and Christian Witt-Dörring and Janis Staggs, eds., *Wiener Werkstätte 1903-1932: The Luxury of Beauty* (Munich: Prestel, 2017).

2 _____ For further details, see Herta Neiß, *Wiener Werkstätte. Zwischen Mythos und wirtschaftlicher Realität* (Vienna: Böhlau, 2014), 72, 134-40; Angela Völker, ed., *Wiener Mode + Modefotografie: Die Modeabteilung der Wiener Werkstätte 1911-1932* (Munich: Schneider-Henn, 1984); Angela Völker, *Die Stoffe der Wiener Werkstätte, 1910-1932* (Vienna: Brandstätter, 1990).

3 _____ Loos also used to write on clothing and critiqued the Wiener Werkstätte frequently for its ornamental, feminine and fashionable traits. See Mark Wrigley, *White Walls, Designer Dresses. The Fashioning of Modern Architecture* (Cambridge, MA: MIT Press, 1995), 77; Jess Berry, *House of Fashion. Haute Couture and the Modern Interior* (London: Bloomsbury Visual Arts, 2018), 86-88.

4 _____ Published in *Hohe Warte* 1, 1904-05. See Noever 2006. Hoffmann had already in 1898 published an article on individuality in dress in Josef Hoffmann, 'Das individuelle Kleid,' *Die Waage*, I., 15 (April 9, 1898): 251-2.

5 _____ According to Traude Hansen, this story was told by former MAK Vienna curator Hans Ankwicz-Kleehoven. See Traude Hansen, *Wiener Werkstätte Mode: Stoffe, Schmuck, Accessoires* (Vienna: Brandstätter, 1984), 40.

6 _____ See *The Sun* (April 16, 1911): 3.

7 _____ After having quit the Wiener Werkstätte, Moser also exhibited dresses together with his wife Ditha at the Kunstgewerbeschau 1908 in Vienna. See Angela Völker, 'Textiles, Fashion, and Theater Costumes,' in *Koloman Moser. Designing Modern Vienna 1897-1907*, ed. Christian Witt-Dörring (Munich: Prestel, 2013), 134.

8 _____ See Janis Staggs, 'The Inside: A Female Realm. Abandoning the Corset to Express Individual Character,' in Christian Witt-Dörring, ed., *Josef Hoffmann: Interiors 1902-1913* (New York: Neue Galerie, 2006), 120.

9 _____ See Noever 2006, 89. There exists also a contemporary book which calls Hoffmann and Moser 'wife dressers', and Klimt too, although he was not married. See 'The Austrian Wife Dressing Husbands' in Lillian Langseth-Christensen, ed., *A Design for Living* (New York: Viking, 1987), 195-225. Likely, a lot of information was lost with Hoffmann's divorce from his first wife Anna Hladik and Moser's early death in 1918.

10 _____ See Dokumentensammlung des Werkbundarchivs, inventory number D 102-6645. Klimt not only had a big interest in his clients' dresses, which is evident in many of his paintings, but he also especially featured Wiener Werkstätte textiles and fashion in his portraits of Friederike Beer-Monti and Johanna Staude. As documented in the magazine *Hohe Warte*, Schwestern Flöge is known to also have collaborated with other artists like Jutta Sika for their dresses. See *Hohe Warte* 5, 2 (1905-06): 78. Unfortunately, the authorship of many dresses Emilie wore cannot be ascertained as there is no archive of the Schwestern Flöge, and hardly any documentation regarding clothing design preceding the Wiener Werkstätte fashion department's opening has survived in the Wiener Werkstätte archive.

11 _____ The cartons for the Stoclet Frieze are today kept at the MAK Vienna. There is evidence that Emilie helped Klimt fill the paint into Klimt's outlines of the drawing. See Wolfgang Georg Fischer, *Gustav Klimt und Emilie Flöge. Genie und Talent, Freundschaft und Besessenheit* (Vienna: Brandstätter 1987), 132.

12 _____ Over the years, Emilie Flöge was gifted many jewellery pieces from Klimt by the Wiener Werkstätte. For more info, see Paul Asenbaum, ed., *Glanzstücke. Emilie Flöge und der Schmuck der Wiener Werkstätte*, exh. cat. (Stuttgart: Arnoldsche Art Publishers, 2008). There were more Wiener Werkstätte items in her estate, like a binder from the Wiener Werkstätte 'Jagdfalke' fabric (Figs. 32 & 33).

13 _____ Angela Völker, 'Textiles, Fashion, and Theater Costumes,' 194-245. Similar ornamented dresses and caftans can be found among the Wiener Werkstätte fashion department's early documented designs.

14 _____ One of them was artist Mileva Roller, as photographed by Madame D'Ora in 1909. See Lara Steinhäußer, 'Women's clothing as another surface: Josef Hoffmann and Fashion,' in *Josef Hoffmann, 1870-1956: Progress through Beauty. The Guide to His Oeuvre*, ed. Christoph Thun-Hohenstein, Matthias Boeckl, Rainald Franz and Christian Witt-Dörring (Birkhäuser Verlag, 2021), 335-340.

15 _____ The coat is documented on a glass-plate negative in the Wiener Werkstätte archive and could recently be identified as Hoffmann's design that is described in detail in the Viennese magazine *Wiener Mode* in 1911. See *Wiener Mode* XXIV, 16, 930.

16 _____ Before that, we can see that the Wiener Werkstätte also used marble effects not only on paper for boxes, fans and paravents, but also for textiles for furniture and blouses. This marble effect was also used for dresses of female figures in wall panels at the boutique of the Flöge sisters and for a paravent (WWPV 830) that was used in the Wiener Werkstätte's own fashion department. See Lara Steinhäußer, 'Transgressive Patterns at the MAK: Transnational and Transmedial Dimensions in the Wiener Werkstätte's Artistic Textiles and Fashion,' in *Tracing Wiener Werkstätte Textiles: Viennese Textiles from the Cotsen Textile Traces Study Collection*, ed. Régine Bonnefoit and Marie-Eve Celio-Scheurer (Basel: Birkhäuser, 2023), 46-49.

17 _____ See Lena Krautgartner, 'Die Schwestern Flöge. Inszenierte Weiblichkeit im Wien des Fin-de-Siécle,' in *Gestalterinnen. Frauen, Design und Gesellschaft im Wien der Zwischenkriegszeit*, ed. Elana Shapira, Anne-Kathrin Rossberg (Berlin: De Gruyter, 2023), 49-64.

18 _____ There are two of these posters inventoried at the MAK – Museum of Applied Arts Vienna as Pl 1496 and Pl 1748. The Österreichische Nationalbibliothek also has the same poster inventoried as Inv. No. PLA16305519 as well as the ALBERTINA Museum in Vienna as DG2003/1731. Among the collection of the MAK, one can also find an invitation for Poiret's Viennese Fashion shows with another one of Lepape's designs from *Les choses de Paul Poiret vues par Georges Lepape* from 1911 on the cover, inventoried as WWGG 566. For further details on the intersections of the Wiener Werkstätte and Poiret, see Lara Steinhäußer, 'Die Wiener Werkstätte und Paul Poiret: Kooperationen, Einflüsse und Differenzen der Wiener und Pariser Mode und ihrer medialen Repräsentation zwischen 1903 und 1932' (Unpublished MA thesis, University of Vienna, 2019) and Heather Hess, 'The Lure of Vienna: Poiret and the Wiener Werkstätte,' in *Poiret*, ed. Harold Koda and Andrew Bolton (Yale University Press, 2007), 39-40.

19 _____ *Neues Wiener Journal* (November 19, 1911): 11 and *Neues Wiener Tagblatt* (November 12, 1911): 12.

20 _____ *Neue Freie Presse* (December 2, 1911): 9-10.

21 _____ In an auction of the estate of Poiret's wife Denise, even knives of the Wiener Werkstätte were sold. See *La création en liberté. L'univers de Paul et Denise Poiret* (Paris: Piasa, 2005), Vol. I, 97.

22 _____ Steinhäußer, 'Women's clothing as another surface,' 338-39. Interestingly, Poiret's villa by architect Louis Süe from 1909 already bore striking similarities to Hoffmann's Palais Stoclet, as Troy has noted elsewhere. See Nancy Troy, *Couture Culture* (Cambridge, MA: MIT Press, 2003), 88-92.

23 _____ Berta Zuckerkandl, 'Paul Poiret und die Klimt-Gruppe,' in *Neues Wiener Journal* (November 25, 1923): 5-6.

24 _____ Eduard Sekler, *Josef Hoffmann. Das architektonische Werk. Monographie und Werkverzeichnis* (Salzburg: Residenz Verlag, 1982), 349.

25 _____ See Paul Poiret, *En habillant l'époque* (Paris: Grasset, 1974), 116.

26 _____ Berta Zuckerkandl, 'Die Wahrheit über Paul Poiret. Anlässlich des Zusammenbruches des Salons, der seinen Namen führt,' in *Neues Wiener Journal* (September 8, 1931): 5.

27 _____ Berta Zuckerkandl, *Österreich intim: Erinnerungen 1892-1942* (Vienna: Amalthea Verlag, 2013), 123-129.

28 _____ Hess, 'The Lure of Vienna,' 40.

29 _____ Lara Steinhäußer, 'Von mustergültigen Ornamenten bis zu fantastischen Kreaturen: Dagobert Peches vernetztes Textilrepertoire,' in *Peche Pop*, ed. Lilli Hollein, Claudia Cavallar and Anne-Katrin Rossberg exh. cat. (Cologne: Walther König, 2024), 232.

30 _____ Bénédicte Gady, 'Dessins de mode de Victor Lhuer,' in Bénédicte Gady, *Le dessin sans réserve. Collections du Musée des Arts Décoratifs*, exh. cat. (Paris: MAD, 2020), 233-235.

31 _____ Steinhäußer, 'Transgressive Patterns at the MAK,' 40-43.

32 _____ Hess, 'The Lure of Vienna,' 40.

33 _____ Völker, 'Die Stoffe der Wiener Werkstätte,' 206-207.

34 _____ See e.g. *Vogue* (May 15, 1913): 23-24, 230-231; *House and Garden* (July 1913): 32-34, 56; *Dry Goods Economist* (April 12, 1913): 37; *Arts and Decoration* (June 1913): 279-81, 290; *Textile Kunst und Industrie*, 6 (1913): 227-242, 270.

35 _____ Hee-Jeong Moon, 'L'École "Martine" de Paul Poiret' in *Une émergence du design. France 20e siècle*, ed. Stéphane Laurent (Paris: Université Paris 1 Panthéon-Sorbonne 2019).

36 _____ Also Zuckerkandl commented on these parallels in her memoirs. See Zuckerkandl 'Österreich intim,' 128.

37 _____ *Table Talk* (October 15, 1925): 20.

38 _____ Arne Sildatke, *Dekorative Moderne: Das Art Déco in der Raumkunst der Weimarer Republik* (Berlin: LIT, 2013), 184.

35

36

35 Josef Hoffmann, 'Kunstschau' armchair, No. 729, made by J. & J. Kohn, c. 1907, MAK – Museum of Applied Arts, Vienna, H 3101.
36 Josef Hoffmann, chair with finger hole, model No. T826, 1914, MAK – Museum of Applied Arts, Vienna, H2301.
37 Guy Pierre Fauconnet for Paul Poiret / Atelier Martine, drawing of an interior with chairs inspired by Hoffmann's chairs Nos. T826 and 729, gouache, Musée de Chelles Alfred-Bonno.
38 Guy Pierre Fauconnet for Paul Poiret / Atelier Martine, drawing of an interior with chairs inspired by Hoffmann's chairs Nos. T826 and 729, gouache, Musée de Chelles Alfred-Bonno.

'My curiosity prompted me to make a special journey to Brussels to see Mr. Stoclet's house, built by the Viennese architect Hoffmann. He had designed not only the house and the outbuildings, but also the garden, the carpets, the furniture, the chandeliers, the plates, the silverware, Mrs. Stoclet's dresses and her husband's walking sticks and neckties. This substitution of the architect's taste for the personality of the proprietors has always seemed to me a sort of slavery – a subjection that makes me smile. My apologies to Mr. and Mrs. Stoclet, who were such magnanimous hosts.'

Model wearing an ensemble by Paul Poiret, leaning on his 'Cambodia' armchair against a background of Atelier Martine wallpaper, photographed by Boris Lipnitzki, 1927.

'J'allai par curiosité à Bruxelles tout exprès pour connaître la demeure de M. Stocklet (sic), construite par l'architecte Hoffmann, de Vienne, qui avait dessiné non seulement la maison et ses dépendances, mais aussi le jardin, les tapis, les meubles, les lustres, les assiettes, l'argenterie, les robes de Madame, les cannes et les cravates de Monsieur. Cette substitution du goût de l'architecte à la personnalité des propriétaires m'a toujours semblé une sorte d'esclavage et de sujétion qui me fait sourire et je m'en excuse auprès de M. et Mme Stocklet (sic) qui furent pour moi des hôtes inoubliables.' (Paul Poiret, *En habillant l'époque*, 1930, 146)

1 Jeanne Lanvin as she leans against the banister with daisy motive in her home on rue Barbet-de-Jouy, which was furnished by Armand-Albert Rateau, photographed by Boris Lipnitzki, 1932.

AT HOME WITH THE DESIGNERS: PAUL POIRET AND JEANNE LANVIN

Jess Berry

When the first credited haute couturier Charles Frederick Worth opened Maison Worth in 1870, he set himself apart from other fashion merchants by devising elaborate aristocratic settings for the reception of his garments. From this point onwards, the interior design of maison premises, retail boutiques and flagship stores has played a significant role in the representation, promotion and consumption of luxury fashion. Throughout fashion history, some of the most celebrated designers of their times have used images of not only their fashion salons and retail environments to promote their collections, but also their private apartments and houses.[1] By collaborating with celebrated *ensembliers* (decorator-architects) in the decoration of both their business premises and their homes, haute couturiers were able to further enhance their reputations as tastemakers at the forefront of style.

During the early twentieth century, the visual spectacle of the confluence between fashion and the interior was disseminated beyond retail environments through publications such as *Vogue*, *Femina*, *Art & Décoration*, and *La Gazette du Bon Ton*, among others. These magazines played a significant role in promoting the aesthetics of modernism to a wider public, and couturiers of this era clearly understood the commercial value of publicising their labels through this medium. Fashion and interior decoration were understood as modes of self-expression and became the 'visual, material and spatial expressions of women's engagement with modernity'.[2] This is significant as historically, modernity has been gendered male.[3] Symbols of modernity – including modern architecture, cities and industrialised production – were ultimately tied to public and institutional structures governed by men that obscured the perspectives and lives of women, who were largely confined to the domestic and private spheres.[4] Publicity of fashionable clothing in the context of domestic spaces was instrumental in educating women that through consumption, luxury connoisseurship could be emulated in their own homes and on their bodies. Consuming fashionable lifestyles was a way for women to embody modernity and display their social and cultural acuity.

Early-twentieth century designers Paul Poiret and Jeanne Lanvin were pioneers in this realm, taking the publicity of their private residencies, salons and boutiques to a new level of sophisticated brand management. They both positioned the interior as an integral element of their fashion houses – conflating the public and private as promotional tools to sell clothing as well as interior décor. Poiret and Lanvin both promoted their brands as lifestyles through their own respective interior-design firms, Atelier Martine and Lanvin Décoration. These two designers set a precedent for other haute couturiers to develop holistic brand identities with shared aesthetics across fashion and the interior. Visually publicising their own homes was central to this endeavour.

The haute couturier Paul Poiret (1879-1944) might be the first fashion designer to create a lifestyle brand.[5] His entrepreneurial acumen for synthesising fashion and the interior to promote his creations in dress, perfumes, cosmetics and home furnishings through illustration and photography offered a new model of publicity that others would follow. In 1911 Poiret opened his design studio Atelier Martine at 107 rue du Faubourg Saint-Honoré to complement his already established fashion maison and perfume store, Rosine. Poiret collaborated with the *ensemblier* Louis Süe to renovate his couture maison and was highly influenced by the Weiner Werkstätte and their philosophy of creating visual unity in the domestic environment, which included harmonising clothing with interior-design elements.[6]

2 Georges Lepape, plate from the album *Les Choses de Paul Poiret vues par Georges Lepape*, 1911, Diktats Bookstore.

3 Paul Poiret, 'Strozzi' gown, autochrome by Jules Gervais-Courtellement, from Paul Cornu, 'L'art de la robe', *Art & Décoration*, April 1911, MoMu, Antwerp, T2022/12.

4 Paul Poiret, gown, photographed in the couture salon on rue d'Antin, featuring a chair upholstered in Atelier Martine furnishing fabric, c. 1920, Musée des Arts Décoratifs, Paris.

5 Atelier Martine for the Société Anonyme des Anciens Établissements Desfossé & Karth, fabric design, gouache on paper, 1919, Musée des Arts Décoratifs, Paris.

Poiret's couture creations were renowned for their 'exotic' influences in silhouette, fabrics and colourways. Matching the aesthetics of his salon décor to his ensembles was an important element of his stylistic vision. A description of the salons printed in the magazine *Le Miroir des Modes,* dating from 1912, highlights how the interiors of the salon are an appropriate backdrop to his orientalist fantasy fashions:

> 'The walls [...], decorated with panels of Nile green, are enriched by frames threaded with dark green and antiqued gold. On the floor, a raspberry-colored carpet, on the windows, taffeta curtains in the same tone. The very clear opposition of these two colors, the one neutral and the other hot, produced a bizarre atmosphere, at once soft and vibrant, and which must harmonize happily with the fresh and buoyant colors from which Poiret likes to take his effects'[7]

The illustrator Georges Lepape – in the pochoir prints created for *Les Choses de Paul Poiret vues par Georges Lepape* (1911) – similarly highlights the continuum between Poiret's fashionable creations and the domestic environment. For example, the second plate of the album (Fig. 2) depicts a model wearing an elegant red empire-line gown sparsely decorated with teal bows and ruffles. These colours can be seen replicated in the raspberry-striped wallpaper glimpsed through a door window, and accented in the teal boiserie, lampshade and soft furnishings that decorate the room. *Art & Décoration* published two coloured photographs of Poiret's models in April 1911. They were realised with the autochrome printing process by the company Photo-Coleur directed by Jules Gervais-Courtellement, and are evidence that Lepape's illustrations are faithful to the colour scheme of the maison (Fig. 3).[8] The accompanying text by Paul Cornu draws attention to the perception that Poiret's fashions were best appreciated 'against a modern décor, where the design of the furniture and the tone of the draperies all reflect the same aesthetic tendencies.'[9]

Maison Paul Poiret served the double function of business and home for the designer, and likely spurred the impetus to conflate the public and private spaces of the maison as a promotional tool for both his fashion and interior-décor businesses. He was careful to align the décor of the salon with the overall schema of his home – a technique that also aided the promotion of Atelier Martine's products. An article in *Vogue* reviewing the newly opened Martine store in 1912 observes, 'to those acquainted with his magnificently appointed suite of salons, decorated and coloured to his unique taste'[10] the new venture is of no surprise. Here, Poiret is positioned as a pioneer of the fashionable interior, where *Vogue* proclaims:

> '[…] certainly couturiers have never before insisted that chairs, curtains, rugs and wall coverings should be considered in the choosing of a dress, or rather that the style of dress should influence the interior decorations of the home'.[11]

Poiret's foray into interior design included: École Martine, an art school for underprivileged girls who often created patterns for textiles; Atelier Martine, the design studio, furniture and decorating service; and La Maison Martine, the shop front for the design studio's products. A 1913 *Vogue* feature on this 'unique Paris shop' praised Poiret's original colour schemes and striking interior-decorating themes that combined 'Byzantine modernised and Frenchified themes'.[12] During the height of its success, Martine sold wallpapers, cushions, rugs, glassware and soft furnishings in its own shops located in France, London and Vienna, as well as in American and German department stores. Martine was also commissioned to decorate a beauty salon for Helena Rubinstein, set designs for theatre, luxury suites for the ocean liner *Île de France* and the interior design of three barges – *Amours* (Fig. 6), *Délices* and *Orgues* – for the Exposition des Arts Décoratifs et Industriels Modernes in 1925.[13]

The reciprocal relationship between fashion and the interior that Poiret cultivated through Martine and his couture house can be further seen in the confluence between textile designs across surfaces. For example, Paul Poiret's jacket from 1924 uses a fauna-and-flora textile design with deer produced by the young women who worked for Martine in 1920 (Fig. 9). This pattern is very similar to a wallpaper print depicted in a dining-room schema by Martine published in the *Intérieurs Français* portfolio of pochoir prints produced by Jean Badovici in 1925 (Fig. 8). This dining-room design is part of a series of Martine interiors including an atrium, staircase, bar, hall, studio and telephone room that featured in the folio, alongside examples by leading French *ensembliers* of the day, including Eileen Gray, Robert Mallet-Stevens, Süe et Mare, Émile-Jacques Ruhlman and André Groult. Martine's contributions to the volume are instantly recognisable for their vibrant saturated-colour palettes, dense patterned surfaces and eclectic mixing of styles.

Pochoir prints such as those created for *Les Choses de Paul Poiret vues par Georges Lepape* and *Intérieurs Français* were an important part of Poiret's marketing strategy. Folios of these prints were produced as luxury catalogues and appealed to haute couturiers and *ensembliers* alike for their ability to represent details of textiles and decorative schemes in faithful colour.[14] For Poiret, because of their expense, quality and artistry, these hand-stencilled prints also represented an opportunity to convey the exclusivity of his designs.[15] While specialised portfolios of prints were limited editions and often sold to couture clientele, they reached a wider audience through reproductions in print magazines of the day, including *Gazette du Bon Ton*, *Femina* and *Art & Décoration*, thus providing Poiret a further avenue to publicise his creations.

Poiret was a master of modern publicity, artfully orchestrating the dissemination of his products through photographs, illustrations and articles that featured in both fashion and design magazines throughout the 1910s and early 1920s (Fig. 10). Denise Poiret, the couturier's wife, muse and mannequin, was the brand's best advertisement. In addition to modelling Poiret fashions at social events, parties and promotional tours, Denise Poiret was often photographed in their home, dressed in her husband's creations and surrounded by Martine furnishings. These promotional images include several photographs by Boris Lipnitzki of Denise in the bedroom, which was decorated with Martine-patterned textiles, floral wallpaper, striped upholstered chairs and black-and-white chequerboard floor (Fig. 12). By using Denise as a model, situated in the private realm of their home, Poiret forged intimate bonds with his clientele, including them in his inner realm through publicity and demonstrating how his fashions might achieve their full effect in the context of Martine decoration. This type of publicity aligned modern fashion with modern lifestyles and fashionable personas. The illustrated press promoted both fashion and interior decoration as an expression of identity by focusing on notable personalities and their unique style. Couturier's homes were photogenic subject matter for consumers of modern fashion and decoration. By publicising his own home as a backdrop to his fashions, Poiret presented a new space for couturiers to promote their brands through a saleable fashion interior. This approach was also influential to Jeanne Lanvin's use of interior décor as the backdrop to her fashions.

The couturier Jeanne Lanvin (1867-1946) began her career as a milliner in 1889 at 22 rue du Faubourg Saint-Honoré. She became a couturier in 1909, with subsequent fashion ventures in children's clothing, womenswear, men's and women's sportswear, and fur. Like Paul Poiret, she recognised the significance of interior design in creating brand identity. She collaborated with the celebrated *ensemblier* Armand-Albert Rateau (1882-1938), who incidentally she met through Poiret, to design the interiors for her Maison salon, boutiques and private residences, as well as to establish an interior-design firm, Lanvin-Décoration.[16]

In 1921 the magazine *Arts & Decoration* reviewed Lanvin's newly opened interior-design store at 15 rue du Faubourg Saint-Honoré. The article commented favourably on the alliance of the pair's two distinct tastes, recognising the fashion designer for her 'creative imagination and breath of modernity' and Rateau for his 'reconstitution of the spirit of a prior age'.[17] This aesthetic collaboration visually combined elements of classical antiquity, Louis XVI French classicism and stylised motifs from nature, along with geometric forms. Lanvin-Décoration sold luxury objects for an elite clientele, including furniture, carpets, rugs, mirrors, objects d'art, wall coverings and moulded boiserie. In addition to private commissions, the pair worked on the interior for the Théâtre Daunou in Paris, Lanvin's *hôtel particulier* at 16 rue Barbet-de-Jouy, and the Pavillon d'Élégance at the *Exposition Internationale des Arts Decoratifs* in 1925. While Lanvin-Décoration only took commissions for four years before folding, it offered Jeanne Lanvin an important further avenue to promote her style to her clients.

Rateau simultaneously undertook the design of the Lanvin boutique refurbishment alongside Lanvin's personal residence in 1921. This included new schemas for her

6 Bedroom on the *Amours* barge furnished by Atelier Martine for l'Exposition des arts décoratifs, photographed by Auguste Léon. 5 October 1925. Musée départemental Albert-Kahn, Archive de la Planète, Boulogne-Billancourt.

7 Paul Poiret for Atelier Martine, large cubic 'Cambodia' armchair in painted wood with wool satin upholstery, c. 1920, Galerie Maxime Flatry.

8 Atelier Martine, dining room with fauna-and-flora wallpaper, stencilling (pochoir) from Jean Badovici, *Intérieurs français*, Éditions Albert Morancé, c. 1925.

9 Paul Poiret and Atelier Martine, fauna-and-flora-print jacket, 1924, Musée des Arts Décoratifs, Paris, UF 64-46-4.

10   Paul Poiret and Atelier Martine, dining room at the exhibition of furniture store Herrmann Gerson in Berlin, from *Deutsche Kunst und Dekoration*, Vol. XVII, November 1913, MoMu, Antwerp.
11   Paul Poiret and Atelier Martine, sleeveless blouse and hat with floral 'Les Roses' embroidery, c. 1915, Palais Galliera, Musée de la Mode de la Ville de Paris.

12 Denise Poiret at home in front of a painting by Kees Van Dongen, c. 1920, photographed by Boris Lipnitzki.

home's reception room, library, gallery and dining room on the first floor, and bedroom, bathroom and boudoir on the second floor. The signature style of Lanvin-Décoration was on display throughout, including classical mouldings depicting scenes from nature, large Coromandel-style lacquer screens adorned with illustrations of woodland animals, furnishings crafted from marble and oak, and wall coverings in Lanvin's signature blue.

Lanvin's fashion designs and her interior-design collaborations with Rateau share an aesthetic sensibility. For example, a cornflower-blue silk chiffon coat, dress and slip (1928) (Fig. 13) featuring layers of concentric circular crochet bear striking compositional resemblance to the silk wall coverings and draperies adorned with white decorative embroidery that completely enveloped the walls of her bedroom (Fig. 14). These wall coverings were created in the atelier at Lanvin-Décoration, which sold similar designs to the public in 1925.[18]

A penchant for decorative embellishment seems to underpin both Lanvin's and Rateau's approach to design. For example, Lanvin's Boulogne beige crepe dress from 1920 (Fig. 15) with its triangle-patterned motifs and pearl embroidery can be seen replicated in the white, black and beige triangular Hauteville marble tiles designed for Lanvin's private bathroom (Fig. 16). The black-and-white triangular motif features several times across Lanvin's collections, including the pénombre beaded gown (1929) and the Oxford dress (1924) with triangle-patterned bell sleeves.[19] The likely source of this reoccurring black-and-white triangular motif is a Japanese fan held in Lanvin's collection of 'exotic' textiles, objects d'art and garments from around the world that influenced and inspired her creations.[20] This 'exotic' influence – common to the designs of many couturiers of the period, not least Poiret – also took form in Lanvin's interiors and similarly reflected Rateau's aesthetic taste. Lanvin's bathroom was resplendent in its use of carved marble for the basin, bath and bidet with fixtures of patinated bronze. The bath alcove was decorated with an impressive plaster-relief depiction of stylised animals. The overall scheme was inspired by Rateau's interest in Persian design and the luxury of Turkish baths.[21]

The 'marguerite' daisy motif is another pattern that features across Lanvin's fashion and interior-design creations. This daisy motif held personal symbolic significance for Lanvin due to its connection with her daughter's name Marguerite Marie-

Blanche, a muse and model to the designer throughout her career. Stylised marguerite embellishments in embroidery, applique, beads and sequins were a common feature across many of Lanvin's fashion collections and made numerous appearances in the décor of her home. In addition to the embroidered wall coverings of her bedroom, Rateau incorporated the marguerite in all manner of decorative modes: giltwood mirror frames, details on door handles, wooden staircase banisters, carved-wood onlays, and marble bas-reliefs (Fig. 1).

Lanvin's *hôtel particulier* served as the inspiration to their final significant collaboration: l'Allée de la Parure in the Grand Palais and the Pavillon d'Élégance at the 1925 *Exposition Internationale des Arts Décoratifs et Industriels Modernes*. This exhibition, which would give birth to the term 'Art Deco', was the hallmark showcase of the French luxury style of the period. A particularly strong relationship between fashion and the interior developed through this exhibition, where both were seen as vehicles of expression for new modern identities and lifestyles. As Henri Bidou explained in his review of the exhibition for *Vogue*: 'Women live as they dress. The living room and the attire are the image of life.'[22] The harmonious effects achieved between fashion and the interior in this exhibition were surely in part due to Lanvin-Decoration's staging.

Rateau's design accents for the exhibition followed those he had created for Lanvin's home. These included a bas-relief forest scene resembling the one in Lanvin's bathroom, replicas of the bronze lamps featured in her boudoir, a dressing table and chairs designed for her bedroom, a bronze patio lounge chair from her terrace and curtains inspired by the striking blue walls of her bedroom.[23] The Pavillon d'Élégance essentially put Lanvin's private interior world on display as the backdrop for salons presented by the couturiers: Worth, Jenny, Callot Sœurs and Jeanne Lanvin. The period's commentary recognised the significance of viewing haute couture in the context of a harmonious mise en scene that women could adopt in their own homes, where the pavilion created the effect of 'a harmonious home among the exquisite furniture of Rateau... worthy of housing the high selection, represented in fashion.'[24] Images of the pavilion were further circulated through the *Gazette du Bon Ton* and *Vogue*, among other fashion and design magazines, providing favourable publicity for Lanvin's couture business.[25]

Despite Poiret's and Lanvin's pioneering roles in lifestyle branding of fashion and the interior, by the close of 1925 Martine had been sold, and Lanvin-Décoration ceased to operate. Poiret was practically bankrupted by the extravagances of the barges *Amours*, *Délices* and *Orgues*, and Lanvin decided to focus on growing her fashion business in menswear, sportswear and fur.[26] In addition, interior-design styles were moving away from nature and the overtly decorative aesthetics that both couturiers had embraced towards more geometric and streamlined forms. Other fashion designers would, however, follow in their footsteps. In the 1930s both Gabrielle Chanel and Elsa Schiaparelli used the domestic interior as part of their self-representation to the public in fashion photography and advertising, and later designers in the 1980s, such as Ralph Lauren and Fendi, would revive lifestyle branding through homewares to new successes. The representation of couturier homes in contemporary luxury branding strategies has also seen a resurgence more recently. Both Chanel and Dior draw on the mythology of their founding designers with flagship stores re-imagining original furnishing and motifs from their homes in retail spaces. The same is true for Lanvin's original Maison at 22 rue du Faubourg Saint-Honoré. Its

13　Jeanne Lanvin, embroidered silk-muslin coat and dress, 1928, Palais Galliera, Musée de la Mode de la Ville de Paris, GAL1985.176.7.
14　Armand-Albert Rateau, Jeanne Lanvin's bedroom, 1925, Musée des Arts Décoratifs, Paris.

127

15 Jeanne Lanvin, 'Djaoni' design sketch, executed as the 'Boulogne' dress, Winter 1920, Lanvin Heritage, Paris.
16 Armand-Albert Rateau, Jeanne Lanvin's bathroom, 1924-1925, Musée des Arts Décoratifs, Paris.

17 Model wearing a Jeanne Lanvin gown, seated on the 'canapé La scène' by Armand-Albert Rateau, photographed by Edward Steichen, *Vogue*, 1 October 1924.
18 Model wearing the 'Phrynée' coat next to an Armand-Albert Rateau chair in Jeanne Lanvin's couture salon, 1928, photographer unknown, Lanvin Heritage, Paris.
19 Model wearing the 'Rozelane' coat next to an Armand-Albert Rateau chair in Jeanne Lanvin's couture salon, 1928, photographer unknown, Lanvin Heritage, Paris.

current interior décor includes a carved mural inspired by Jeanne Lanvin's bathroom designed by Rateau as well as a black-and-white carpet that references to the original tiled marble floor, and a mural of woodland animals representative of the style of Lanvin-Décoration also features in the flagship store. As in the early twentieth century, the publicity of fashion designers' homes in avenues such as *The World of Interiors* and *Vogue* continues to act as an important indicator of designers' relationship to connoisseurship, thus encouraging the fashion-forward consumer to emulate their style.

Endnotes

1 _____ This essay is adapted from my book *House of Fashion: Haute Couture and the Modern Interior* (London: Bloomsbury, 2018).
2 _____ Penny Sparke, *The Modern Interior* (London: Reaktion, 2008), 75.
3 _____ Elizabeth Wilson, *Adorned in Dreams: Fashion and Modernity* (London: Virago Press, 1983).
4 _____ Rita Felski, *The Gender of Modernity* (Cambridge, MA: Harvard University Press, 1995).
5 _____ Harold Koda and Andrew Bolton, 'Preface: The Prophet of Simplicity,' in *Poiret*, ed. Harold Koda and Andrew Bolton (New York: The Metropolitan Museum of Art, 2007), 13–14.
6 _____ Jared Goss, 'Paul Poiret and the Decorative Arts,' in Koda and Bolton, *Poiret*, 43–44.
7 _____ 'Poiret: Une Silhouette Parisienne,' *Le Miroir des Modes* 64, no. 6 (June 1912): 242, cited in Nancy Troy, *Couture Culture* (Cambridge, MA: MIT Press: 2003), 67–69.
8 _____ Sylvie Lécallier, 'Paul Poiret et le pouvoir de la photographer,' in Lemoine et al., *Le Paris de la modernité, 1905-1925* (Paris: Paris Musées: 2023), 107.
9 _____ Paul Cornu, 'L'Art de la Robe.' *Art & Décoration* (April, 1911): 103–107.
10 _____ 'Poiret's New Kingdom,' *Vogue USA* (July 1912): 16.
11 _____ 'Poiret's New Kingdom,' *Vogue USA*.
12 _____ 'The Shop of Martine,' *Vogue USA* (July 1913): 44.
13 _____ Goss, 'Paul Poiret and the Decorative Arts,' in Koda and Bolton, *Poiret*, 43–44.
14 _____ Jeremy Aynsley, 'Pochoir Prints: Publishing the Designed Interior,' in *Moderne: Fashioning the French Interior*, ed. Marianne Lamonica (New York: Princeton Architectural Press, 2008), 9–32.
15 _____ Troy, *Couture Culture*.
16 _____ Hélène Géuné, *Décoration et haute couture: Armand Albert Rateau pour Jeanne Lanvin, un autre Art déco* (Paris: Les Arts Décoratifs, 2006).
17 _____ Leo Randole, 'An Artist in Dress and Decoration: The entry of Jeanne Lanvin into a new field,' *Art & Decoration* (October 1921): 384.
18 _____ Géuné, *Décoration et haute couture*.
19 _____ Dean Merceron, *Lanvin* (New York: Rizzoli, 2007).
20 _____ Merceron, *Lanvin*.
21 _____ Géuné, *Décoration et haute couture*.
22 _____ Henri Bidou, 'A l'Exposition internationale des arts décoratifs et industriels modernes. Le Décor de la vie moderne,' *Vogue* (August 1, 1925): 29-37, 35, cited in Simon Dell, 'The Consumer and the Making of the *Exposition des Arts Décoratifs et Industriels Modernes*, 1907-1925,' *Journal of Design History* 12, no. 4 (1999): 311–325.
23 _____ Albert Flament, 'Le Pavillon de l'Élégance,' *La Rennaissance de l'art français et des industries de luxe* (July 1925): 303–317.
24 _____ Lucy Neumeyer, 'Le Pavillon de l'Élégance,' *L'Illustration* (August 1925): 25.
25 _____ *Le Pavillon de l'Élégance. L'Exposition des arts décoratifs et industriels modernes, Numéro spécial de la Gazette de Bon Ton*, no. 5 (1925); Henri Bidou, 'À l'Exposition internationale des arts décoratifs et industriels modernes': 29–37.
26 _____ Goss, 'Paul Poiret and the Decorative Arts,' in *Poiret*, ed. Harold Koda and Andrew Bolton (New York: The Metropolitan Museum of Art, 2007), 43–44.; Géuné, *Décoration et haute couture*.

The living room of Yves Saint Laurent and Pierre Bergé, 55 rue de Babylone in Paris, 1984, photographed by François Halard.

Yves Saint Laurent at home in Paris, photographed by Horst P. Horst, *Vogue*, 1 November 1971.

The fireplace in Coco Chanel's private apartment, 31 rue du Cambon in Paris, 1985, photographed by François Halard.

The salon in Coco Chanel's private apartment, 31 rue du Cambon in Paris, 1985, photographed by François Halard.

p.136 Hydrangeas from Dries Van Noten's garden at his home Ringenhof in Lier, photographed by François Halard, *Vogue*, March 2014.

p.137 The red salon in Dries Van Noten's home Ringenhof in Lier, photographed by François Halard, *Vogue*, March 2014.

Karl Lagerfeld's apartment in Monaco, furnished with Memphis Milano designs, photographed by Jacques Schumacher for *Mode und Wohnen*, January 1983.

Karl Lagerfeld at a table in his 'Memphis' apartment in Monaco, photographed by Jacques Schumacher for *Mode und Wohnen*, January 1983.

Dirk Van Saene and Walter Van Beirendonck at home, photographed by Alexander Popelier, *Knack Weekend*, August 2018.

Dirk Van Saene's studio, photographed by Alexander Popelier, *Knack Weekend*, August 2018.

p. 142   The living room in the London home of Faye Toogood and Matt Gibberd designed by Walter Segal, photographed by Henry Bourne, 2019.

p. 143   Faye Toogood in bed, photographed by Henry Bourne, 2019.

'Ladies fashion!
You disgraceful chapter in
the history of civilisation!
You tell of mankind's
secret desires. Whenever
we peruse your pages,
our souls shudder at the
frightful aberrations.'

'Damenmode! Du gräßliches kapitel kulturgeschichte! Du erzählst von der menschheit geheimen lüsten. Wenn man in deinen Seiten blättert, erbebt die seele angesichts der fürchterlichen verirrungen und unerhörten laster.' (Adolf Loos, 'Dokumente der Frauen', themanummer *Frauenkleidung*, no. 23, 1 March 1902)

145

Adolf Loos wearing a frock coat, c. 1904, photographed by Otto Mayer, Österreichische Nationalbibliothek, Bildarchiv Austria, Pf 830 : D ⊕.

'When I was finally commissioned to build a house, I said to myself: the external appearance of a house can only be changed as much as a tailcoat. So not much. [...] One thing I knew: in order to continue the line of the development, I had to go for a greater degree of simplicity. I had to replace the gold buttons with black ones. The house had to be unobtrusive.'

'Als mir nun endlich die aufgabe zuteil wurde, ein haus zu bauen, sagte ich mir: Ein haus kann sich in der äußeren erscheinung höchstens wie der frack verändert haben. Also nicht viel. [...] Eines wußte ich: ich mußte, um in der linie der entwicklung zu bleiben, noch bedeutend einfacher werden. Die goldenen knöpfe mußte ich durch schwarze ersetzen. Unauffällig muß das haus aussehen.'
(Adolf Loos, 'Architectuur', in *Der Sturm*, no. 42, 15 December 1910)

Adolf Loos, Villa Müller, photographed by Martin Gerlach, c. 1930, the ALBERTINA Museum, Vienna, ALA5016.

Adolf Loos, mahogany and silk velvet 'Knieschwimmer' armchair for Kapsa Villa in Prague, made by Vereinigte U.P. Werke, Brno, Czechoslovakia, c. 1930, private collection, Galerie Yves Macaux, Vienna.

Adolf Loos, interior of Dr. Frantisek and Milada Müller's Villa Müller in Prague, photographed by Martin Gerlach, c. 1930, the ALBERTINA Museum, Vienna, ALA2488.

'Fashion today
has no style;
it is always merely
fashionable.'

'Die heutige Mode hat keinen Stil,
sie ist immer nur modisch.'
(Lilly Reich, 'Modefragen', *Die Form: Monatsschrift für gestaltende Arbeit*, 1, no. 5, 1.1922, 8)

Lilly Reich, dress made of black rep, 1926, photographed by N. and C. Hess, from Else Hoffmann, 'Von Wäsche und Kleidern', *Neue Frauenkleidung und Frauenkultur* 22, No. 3 or 4, 1926, Von Parish Kostümbibliothek, Munich.

1   Lilly Reich, quilted jacket in yellow Shantung silk, 1926, photographed by N. and C. Hess, from Else Hoffmann, 'Von Wäsche und Kleidern', *Neue Frauenkleidung und Frauenkultur 22*, No. 3 or 4, 1926, Von Parish Kostümbibliothek, Munich.

INTERWEAVING FASHION AND THE INTERIOR: THE MATERIALITY OF LILLY REICH'S MODERN DESIGN

Robin Schuldenfrei

The intersection of fashion, gender, and the modern interior is uniquely evident in the creative output of Lilly Reich, whose keen talent in multiple fields mutually informed and enhanced her resulting design work. Her use of striking materials, diverse textures and dramatic draping was carefully staged in spaces of radically new modernism. Reich was a polyvalent designer of clothing, window displays, exhibition installations, domestic interiors and furniture. She also engaged in critically rethinking the modes of production to achieve her results and impact the field of modern fashion and architecture.

Berlin-born Reich trained in embroidery and, after journeying to Vienna in 1908, worked in the studio of Josef Hoffmann. Upon her return to Berlin, she became a student of Else Oppler-Legband, a prominent creative leader and early member of the influential Deutscher Werkbund, the prominent alliance of designers, businessmen and government figures committed to raising design standards in Germany. Through Oppler-Legband, Reich gained entry into a prominent design circle of leading Werkbund figures such as Hermann Muthesius and Peter Behrens. When the Werkbund opened a school for display-window decoration in 1910 under the directorship of Oppler-Legband, preeminent practitioners in the field were brought in, including Reich. This early involvement with the modern tools and techniques of the display window – the schematic display of wares, advertising-poster design, and the use of technology, perspective and architecture – would inform Reich's subsequent interior work. Simultaneously, Reich was working on clothing displays for the Wertheim department store, one of the largest and most notable stores in Berlin. As early as 1912, Reich was established enough as a designer in her own right that she was one of the very few women offered membership to the Werkbund by its board of directors. By 1914, at the age of 29, she had opened her own independent fashion atelier (Figs. 1-3). In 1920 she was the first woman elected to the governing board of the Werkbund. By the early 1920s, Reich had a flourishing creative practice in Berlin producing clothing designs and accessories, window displays, exhibition installations, and interiors that included furniture and finishings.

QUESTIONS OF FASHION

In this period, Reich was active in designing original garments but, crucially, she also developed carefully argued theories regarding the place of fashion in contemporary culture. In a groundbreaking article, 'Questions of Fashion' (1922), Reich introduced readers of the journal *Die Form* to recent developments in the design of clothing in relation to problems of the age.[1] Reich, who by then had a long-established Berlin atelier, succinctly contextualised issues relevant beyond the comparatively narrow field of fashion, issues that were mainstays for modern designers and groups such as the Werkbund. She advocated for women to consume genuine German fashion rather than domestically produced, inexpensive copies and imports from Paris. Reich called for each woman 'to be what she is' and not 'to appear as what she is not'.[2] At times, the reform ideals of the Werkbund were as much ideological as material- or design-driven. Reich's was a crucial voice in those period debates.

In her article, Reich superimposes onto questions of fashion a layered and vivid image of the rapid change the period was going through in the fields of industry, finance and society. At the time of writing, 1922, Germany was still recovering from the First World War and experiencing the devastating effects of the inflation of its currency due to war reparations. This spirit

2   Lilly Reich, morning dress, white wool crepe with embroidered sleeves, 1926, photographed by N. and C. Hess, from Else Hoffmann, 'Von Wäsche und Kleidern', *Neue Frauenkleidung und Frauenkultur* 22, No. 3 or 4, 1926, Von Parish Kostümbibliothek, Munich.
3   Lilly Reich, brown ribbed wool dress, 1926, from F. S., 'Angelika an Ursula', *Neue Frauenkleidung und Frauenkultur* 22, No. 1, 1926.

4   Lilly Reich and Ludwig Mies van der Rohe, glass room for *Die Wohnung* (The Dwelling) exhibition, Stuttgart, 1927, photographed by Walter Lutkat, from Arthur Korn, *Glas: im Bau und als Gebrauchsgegenstand*, 1929.

5   Lilly Reich, wood exhibit for the materials section of the *Deutsche Bauausstellung* (German Building Exhibition) Berlin, 1931, photographed by Curt Rehbein, Mies van der Rohe Archive, Museum of Modern Art, New York.

6 Lilly Reich, Erdgeschosswohnhaus (Ground-floor House) at 'Die Wohnung unserer Zeit' (The Dwelling of Our Time), *Deutsche Bauausstellung* (German Building Exhibition), photograph of the lady's bedroom, 1931, Mies van der Rohe Archive, Museum of Modern Art, New York.

of the times comes through in her essay's underlying nationalist tone, and yet Berlin was simultaneously becoming a thriving metropolis that would reach its cultural and industrial zenith by the late 1920s.

Reich's article considers stylistic issues and questions of modern production, criticising the widespread use of imitative materials and superficial construction techniques, modern business practices and the rapid pace of change as they manifested themselves especially acutely in clothing design. Reich calls for more self-assuredness on the part of German design: she advocates for a slow and steady organic development that is less wasteful, less dependent on Paris for trends and sales, less snobbish, less a 'slave of supply and demand', and yet still able to stand up to the pressures of the market. Fashion should remain 'attractive and charming' but also functional, accepting of the need for mass production without giving up the role of handcraftsmanship or denigrating it through machine imitation.

Many of Reich's ideas in 'Questions of Fashion' are exemplified by her own clothing design, which was simple, even dowdy compared to contemporary Parisian wares, but which evinced careful attention to materials and craftsmanship, especially in its fine details.

Two years earlier, Reich had demonstrated these ideas in her selection of the best examples of Germany's fashion and accessories for the exhibition *Fashion Craft*, held at the Arts and Crafts Museum in Berlin, which brought together artisans and large-scale firms.[3] She articulated industry's economic constraints, namely supply and demand, and the pressure to present new designs each season – while describing the individual craftsman at work, in William Morrisesque terms, as an artist who is propelled by a 'love of material, joy in work, will to form, and not practical and economic considerations'.[4] Reich lamented industry's 'tasteless', 'barbarian misuse' of handicraft, and contended that technology and materials needed to be reconciled.[5] Reich concluded with a call for the handicraft artist to join the factory workshop in order to reach an understanding of industrial processes and to positively influence the designs that would ultimately be produced by machines.[6] Reich thus illuminates a key problem of the age, for fashion and interior design alike: aesthetic form in light of economic and modern manufacturing realities. Although her calls are discussed here in the context of fashion, they chime with design reform in other creative fields, fields in which she also practiced.

BAMBERG METALLWERKSTÄTTEN · BERLIN-NE

			L	N	CHR
MR 1		**Hocker**			
	1/1	Eisengarnstoff	23.-	30.-	36.-
	1/2	Rindleder	36.-	42.-	50.-
	1/3	Korbgeflecht	31.-	37.-	44.-
MR 10		**Stuhl**			
	10/1	Eisengarnstoff	34.-	44.-	54.-
	10/2	Rindleder	48.-	58.-	68.-
	10/3	Korbgeflecht	42.-	53.-	64.-
MR 20		**Sessel**			
	20/1	Eisengarnstoff	56.-	78.-	95.-
	20/2	Rindleder	75.-	96.-	115.-
	20/3	Korbgeflecht	69.-	92.-	105.-
MR 30		**Stuhl**			
	30/3	Korbgeflecht	66.-	84.-	98.-
	30/4	Kissen in Pflanzendaunen mit kar. Leinen (blau/weiß, blau/gelb, blau/rot)	108.-	122.-	135.-
	30/5	desgl. mit einfarb. Halbleinen, blau, gelb und beige	122.-	136.-	150.-
MR 40		**Sessel**			
	40/3	Korbgeflecht	84.-	120.-	132.-
	40/4	Kissen in Pflanzendaunen mit kar. Leinen (blau/weiß, blau/gelb, blau/rot)	132.-	155.-	175.-
	40/5	desgl. mit einfarb. Halbleinen, blau, gelb und beige	147.-	171.-	192.-
MR 50		**Sessel**			
	50/5	Stoffpolster	95.-	111.-	123.-
	50/6	Lederpolster	105.-	123.-	135.-
	50/7	Pergamentpolster	140.-	156.-	168.-
MR 60		**Sessel aus Stahlrohr**			
	60/3	Korbgeflecht	90.-	105.-	118.-
	60/4	Kissen in Pflanzendaunen mit kar. Leinen (blau/weiß, blau/gelb, blau/rot)	126.-	140.-	153.-
	60/5	desgl. mit einfarb. Halbleinen, blau, gelb, beige	140.-	153.-	165.-
MR 70		**Sessel, Flachstahl**			
	70/8	Stoffkissen	320.-	430.-	480.-
	70/9	Schweinslederkissen	500.-	580.-	650.-

Zeichenerklärung: L = farbig lackiert gelb, rot, blau; N =

Liste 11. X. 31.

7 Bamberg Metallwerkstätten, illustrated product and price list of furniture designed by Ludwig Mies van der Rohe and Lilly Reich, 1931.

LN • LICHTENRADER STRASSE 32 • FERNSPRECHER: F2 NEUKÖLLN 1122

		L	N	CHR				L	N	CHR
Hocker, *Flachstahl*					LR 500		**Tisch**			
8	Stoffkissen	240.-	280.-	300.-		500/1	Sperrholzplatte	46.-	56.-	68.-
9	Schweinslederkissen	310.-	350.-	370.-						
Sessel, *Flachstahl*					LR 510		**Tisch**			
8	Stoffkissen	400.-	460.-	500.-		510/1	Sperrholzplatte	42.-	48.-	57.-
9	Schweinslederkissen	450.-	485.-	520.-						
Liegestuhl					LR 520		**Blumentisch**			
4	Kissen mit Gummibezug	190.-	210.-	230.-		520/1	Kristallglasplatte	57.-	66.-	75.-
Liegestuhl					LR 530		**Kleiner Tisch**			
4	Kissen mit Gummibezug	200.-	220.-	240.-		530/1	Kristallglasplatte	45.-	55.-	65.-
Stuhl					LR 600		**Bett**			
	Stoffpolster	120.-	128.-	136.-		600/1	Stahlmatratze	115.-	150.-	180.-
	Lederpolster	175.-	185.-	195.-		600/2	Gummibänder	140.-	170.-	198.-
Tisch, *60 cm Durchm.*					LR 610		**Couch**			
	Sperrholzplatte	57.-	66.-	75.-		610/1	Stahlmatratze	110.-	140.-	170.-
	Kristallglasplatte	60.-	69.-	78.-		610/2	Gummibänder	135.-	160.-	190.-
	Schwarzglasplatte	75.-	85.-	93.-						
Tisch, *70 cm Durchm.*					LR 620		**Couch**			
	Sperrholzplatte	63.-	72.-	81.-		620/1	Stahlmatratze	100.-	125.-	150.-
	Kristallglasplatte	68.-	77.-	86.-		620/2	Gummibänder	125.-	155.-	180.-
	Schwarzglasplatte	98.-	108.-	118.-						
Tisch, *Flachstahl*										
	Palisanderplatte	265.-	280.-	300.-							
	Kristallglasplatte	420.-	440.-	460.-							
	Schwarzglasplatte	520.-	560.-	600.-							

elt; CHR = verchromt • Alle Modelle sind patentamtlich geschützt

Mit dieser Preisliste verlieren die alten Listen ihre Gültigkeit

FASHION, DESIGN AND THE WERKBUND

The issues Reich raises in her writing and in her creative work in this period take fashion as a starting point but quickly move to the larger Werkbund preoccupations of manufacturing, economy, and quality of domestic design in an ever increasingly international market. Her input was influential because she straddled the spheres of fashion, interior design, exhibition design and critical Werkbund debates. Members of the Werkbund sought to contend with the realities of their age while channelling practitioners towards the desired outcome: the production of well-designed, high-quality goods. The situation that Reich laments in clothing production – surrogate materials and 'sham solutions', thoughtlessly and superficially applied decoration or ornament, cheap imitations of quality design – was analogous to the shortcomings in the production of other types of objects such as furniture and household goods, namely the production of the so-called 'cheap and nasty' machine-made articles that Werkbund designers sought to address. Attention to organic and honest form, ideals which had already been articulated by nineteenth- and early-twentieth-century dress reform movements, was given new urgency with Werkbund concerns about taste and the effects of inexpensive mass production.

Werkbund members polemically positioned the concept of Style ('*Stil*') against that of Fashion ('*Mode*'). Style was seen as capturing the true common spirit of the age and also described a positive theory of form in contradistinction to what the Werkbund viewed as the culturally hostile influence of the capitalist commercial economy.[7] Fashion was Style's antithesis, describing – and not only in clothing – the quick production and turnover of consumer commodities.[8] Reich voices these crucial Werkbund concerns in 'Questions of Fashion' when she writes, 'Fashion from the previous eras had style, since it grew out of long-existent living conditions and societal prerequisites. […] Fashion today has no style; it is merely always fashionable.'[9] One solution, put forth by the Werkbund for many categories of objects and by Reich for fashion, was to resort to standard types ('*Typisierung*') for which appropriate forms could be developed, something that she argued was evidenced in street clothes and sportswear.[10]

Werkbund protagonists were not the first to address the problems posed by fashion for design and society. Prominent architects, cultural critics and theorists such as Heinrich Hübsch, Gottfried Semper, Adolf Loos, Ferdinand Tönnies, Werner Sombart and Georg Simmel all wrote with concern about fashion and the general rapid (over-)production of cheap goods and the effects of accelerated capitalism on an eagerly consuming, undiscerning mass public. The unease about the fast pace of change in clothing production was symptomatic of a more general deep apprehension concerning the acceleration of modern life; mapped onto fashion – a prime mode by which such concerns could be literally and figuratively embodied – were the same anxieties about identity that were expressed about the conditions of modernity more widely. Reich sought to identify what women are – objectively, spiritually, nationally – and then to find forms of clothing that reflect those traits. She turned her attention to one of the areas which she, at that point in her career, knew best: the economy and production of fashion. With conviction, she provided a view into the issues of the day and the terms of the debate in a concise and approachable format that has wider ramifications for considering the development of modernism in 1920s Germany.

10 Ludwig Mies van der Rohe and Lilly Reich, Velvet and Silk Café at *Die Mode der Dame* (Women's Fashion exhibition), Berlin, Germany, 1927, Mies van der Rohe Archive, Museum of Modern Art, New York.

11 Ludwig Mies van der Rohe and Lilly Reich, Velvet and Silk Café at *Die Mode der Dame* (Women's Fashion exhibition), 1927, photographed by Sasha Stone / Globophot Pressedienst, Berlin.

12 Ludwig Mies van der Rohe and Lilly Reich, Velvet and Silk Café at *Die Mode der Dame* (Women's Fashion exhibition), 1927, colour reproduction by Enrique Colomés.

THE EXHIBITION OF MODERN LIFE

Reich possessed a rare combination of artistic and organizational skills which allowed her to maintain an active atelier but also oversee the timely construction and outfitting of major exhibitions, the scale of which required contact with – and coordination of – a vast number of participants. Early career highlights include her participation in a number of exhibitions showcasing the work of women, such as the concept and design participation in *Woman at Home and at Work* (1912), which featured her model apartment for a working-class family and two stores, and the *House of Women* at the 1914 Werkbund exhibition in Cologne, for which she designed the vitrines for shopping arcades. From 1924 to 1926, she worked for the Werkbund House in Frankfurt, selecting objects and organising the displays representing the Werkbund and German design at the Frankfurt International Fair. She also relocated her own atelier from Berlin to Frankfurt during those years.

This previous experience in exhibition design would be the foundation for the leap in creativity and organizational scale her work would take when she entered in an artistic and personal partnership with the architect Ludwig Mies van der Rohe, whom she met in 1924 while in Frankfurt and with whom she moved back to Berlin. This fruitful collaboration resulted in Reich producing the highly innovative modern exhibition layouts and installations for which she is renowned. Her solo projects and the work undertaken together with Mies ushered in a period of dynamic use of materials, new forms and conceptions of space, and new models for dwelling, as can be seen in the large-scale exhibitions that displayed full-scale living spaces and modern industrial products. Projects included *The Dwelling* (1927), organised by the Werkbund, with Reich's exhibition hall of technological appliances and modern furniture. It accompanied the Weissenhof Housing Settlement in Stuttgart, a full-scale housing development organised by Mies for which Reich also contributed to the outfitting of several of the interiors (Fig. 4), the Barcelona Pavilion (1929) and the *German Building Exhibition* in Berlin (1931). There, Mies and Reich presented exhibition houses that showcased modernism at its most sumptuous and Reich organised and designed a 'Material Show' featuring displays of interior and building materials such as furnishing textiles, varieties of glass, floor coverings and wood specimens (Fig. 5). Reich's Ground Floor House in the same exhibition featured a luxurious and highly impractical bedroom furnished with a sumptuous white carpet, a light-coloured upholstered chair, a tubular-steel bed, and a glass-topped, tubular-steel bedside table (Fig. 6). Mies and Reich were able to showcase

13 Lilly Reich, leather, teak and steel daybed No. 258, designed in 1930, produced by Knoll (under the name of Ludwig Mies van der Rohe), 1960s. Interiors Akanthos, Antwerp.

163

14　Ludwig Mies van der Rohe, tubular-steel-and-leather MR 10/2, 1927, Vitra Design Museum, Weil am Rhein, MST-1095-1.

their exacting ideas about materiality and dwelling in full-scale exhibition architecture which allowed them the freedom to express their creativity and present their ideas about modern living without the constriction of client taste or domestic habits.[11] Their lavish, large-scale exhibitions of the 1920s sought to introduce the public to new, modern architecture and interiors. These popular events drew large numbers of visitors and were covered extensively in the press. They deployed two modes of display: large-scale exhibition halls featuring modern products organised by material or object type, and stand-alone, fully furnished show houses through which visitors could walk and admire the contents.

Mies and Reich's collaborative projects, especially their interiors, presented alluring modernist materiality and the luxury of modern architecture.[12] Whether in the design of large-scale family villas or in showcasing modern dwelling ideals through exhibitions for the general public, Mies and Reich expressed ideas about modern interiors through individual materials, giving careful attention to their substance and their surfaces alike. Emphasising a rigorous solidity in their carefully selected and precisely placed materials, Mies and Reich, working together, contrasted the presence of materiality in solid planes of onyx and travertine with thin surface treatments of zebrawood veneer or chromium-plated cruciform columns. Yet they also celebrated the immateriality and the ephemeral qualities of materials such as spare, blank walls; the transparency or semitransparency of various varieties of glass (white milk glass, green or black glass); and the layering of velvet, silk and tulle in their window treatments. The furniture and furnishings, especially the textiles and rugs, with their highly attuned colours and textures, were often Reich's design outright, or were very much indebted to her input and the pair's collaborative design process, even when they were singularly attributed to Mies. Rather than using materials to express concepts of mass production, industry or technology, as many of their peers did, Mies's architectural materials and Reich's furnishing fabrics were statements of modern elegance and luxury. They used these materials to deploy luxury within the visual and theoretical paradigm of modernism and toward social, cultural *and* architectural ends.

COLLABORATIVE FURNITURE DESIGN

The pair also forayed into the wider production of furniture designs that had grown out of domestic house commissions, working closely with the company Bamberg Metallwerkstätten in Berlin. The firm produced a catalogue sheet with the entire collection of Mies and Reich-designed furniture, each piece depicted in outline, accompanied by a listing of the available colours, metals, materials and prices (Fig. 7). Seating coverings were available in a range of materials including cowhide, pigskin, the iconic caning and the more pedestrian two-cord yarn fabric, as well as in plain and checkered linen; tabletops were available in rosewood, plywood, and in clear and black glass. An 'MR' or 'LR' prefix code identified the designer as Mies or Reich. The sheet lists seven pieces of furniture designed by Reich: four tables, a bed and two couches.

The arrangement with the Bamberg Metallwerkstätten was short-lived, superseded by a contract with the major international furniture firm Thonet, which Mies signed in November 1931.[13] Importantly, Thonet produced three pieces of furniture by Reich – a bed and two couches – which only appeared in their first catalogue and were credited to Mies.[14] Reich presumably agreed to, and did not mind, this omission because of her intertwined collaboration with Mies during these years. Given the number of beds and couches Reich was designing in this period, it is instructive to look at her daybed (Fig. 13), an amalgam of the two and a furniture type that worked well in the modern interiors that Mies and Reich were collaborating on. This daybed, credited to Mies but more accurately attributed to Reich, was widely used in commissions (Crous and Philip Johnson apartments (Fig. 15), Villa Wolf, and the Berlin Building Exhibition).[15] Rising on four tubular-steel legs and set on a steel-and-wood frame, this flexible furniture form provided multi-functional uses: daytime seating or resting, and guest bedding.

TEXTILES AS ARCHITECTURE

The evocative effects of materiality as a surface and as a space-defining medium – as interior architecture – receives perhaps its purest expression in Mies and Reich's use of textiles. Via drapes, they created the possibility for interior structure within the open plan, and in this way, their use of textiles can be understood as architectural. This is particularly notable in their major commission, the Tugendhat House (1928-30) in Brno, Czech Republic. Designed in close collaboration, the house's materiality is constituted by the pair's merging of modern form with materialised surface. The textiles selected by Reich form a major component of the interior: the large main floor's open plan could be flexibly closed off into more private spaces through the use of curtains. Layering rich materiality, she double-hung a thin, semi-transparent floor-to-ceiling silk curtain directly in front of a window, followed by velvet or opaque dark drapes, resulting in an interior that created an intimate feeling of contained space, *Raumgefühl*, while simultaneously literally and figuratively enveloping the dweller in material luxury. The drapes of the Tugendhat House, with their interplay of differing surfaces, added subtle surface texture to this spatial definition. A white velvet curtain was placed between the entrance area and the library beyond while a black Shantung silk curtain was hung in front of the conservatory, with a black velvet curtain placed beside it and a silver-gray Shantung silk framing the main glass wall (Fig. 8).[16] Museum of Modern Art curator and architect Philip Johnson described the effect: 'At night raw silk curtains cover the glass walls from floor to ceiling, enhancing the luxuriousness of the interior by their colour and texture. […] The elegance of this room derives not only from its size and the simple beauty of its design, but from the contrast of rich materials and the exquisite perfection of details.'[17] By the late 1920s, artificial silks were readily available on the mass market. Concurrently – and in contrast – expansive swaths of nubby, raw silk were to be found in the interiors of the Tugendhat house, an expressive and expensive detail. Thus, a luxurious yet subtle surface materiality came into play via the sheen of the thin raw silk against the thickness of the velvet curtains' pile. Reich's extensive experience with fabric would have greatly informed both the selection of materials and the implementation of their architectural effects.

Likewise, the Tugendhat House's elegant floor coverings played up their material effect via subtly differing surfaces. The hand-woven light-coloured wool carpet laid on white linoleum in front of the onyx wall in the main living space and the interplay of white lambskins placed on travertine upstairs gave paramount importance to surface texture (Fig. 9). While in some instances the contrast in materials was subtle, often it was vividly distinctive – between hard and soft materials, or vibrant and muted colours (cherry red and apple green versus pale grey and soft pink). Each material selected by Reich was seemingly a part of the whole yet was also legible as an independent, distinctive element within the interior.

The rich structure-giving quality of fabric was celebrated by Mies and Reich in their design of the Velvet and Silk Café (1927) for the Women's Fashion exhibition in Berlin, their most striking work in using textiles as architecture. The enclosing space was entirely structured by hanging lengths of velvet and silk fabric (Fig. 10).[18] To form the café, fabric literally became modernism's curtain 'walls' in draped silk (gold, silver, lemon-yellow and black) and velvet (black, red and orange) (Fig. 12). In harmony with the undulating materials making up the walls, the seats and backrests of Mies's cantilevered chairs (Fig. 14) were formed of spanned material. The overall effect was that nothing was fixed – the space's architecture was constituted and defined by fluidity, resulting in a subjective architectural experience formed by the delicate interplay of material surfaces.

The quality and innovation of the major exhibitions and interiors Reich produced in collaboration with Mies overshadow her prior and later independent work. Although the Museum of Modern Art in New York holds more than 900 of her drawings, the full extent of Reich's creative work will never be known due to the bombing of her studio in 1943 and the omission of credit for work done in collaboration with Mies, a regrettably standard practice at the time. After Mies emigrated to the US without her, their correspondence charts the years that she worked tirelessly with lawyers to protect Mies's patents and managed his contracts with Thonet, his revenue from furniture royalties and his bank account.[19]

Lilly Reich's interior designs and furniture – both in collaboration with Mies and independently – are a major contribution to modernism. Her work as a groundbreaking female designer stands out in a field of male practitioners. Her deft interweaving of the materials of fashion – diaphanous silks, rich velvets, silvery suedes – with the modern luxury of the period interiors in glass and steel resulted in an architecture of elegant modern life. The spaces she created were meant to open up new ideas of living, new freedoms for women that Reich herself embodied as a busy creative professional, and contemporary theories of production and consumption which she formulated through her writing. Reich responded to questions about how modern life's materiality might be conceived with affirmative answers in the form of interiors of striking originality.

15   Ludwig Mies van der Rohe and Lilly Reich, interior of Philip Johnson's apartment in New York, 1930, photographed by Seidman, Mies van der Rohe Archive, Museum of Modern Art, New York.

16   Editorial *Eternal Optimism* with chairs by Ludwig Mies van der Rohe, photographed by Craig McDean for *Vogue*, April 2012.
17   Rachel Weisz in a jumpsuit by Salvatore Ferragamo, sitting on Ludwig Mies van der Rohe's MR 10/2 chair, photographed by Craig McDean for *T Magazine*, May 2019.

Endnotes

1 _____ Lilly Reich, 'Modefragen,' *Die Form* 1, no. 5 (1922): 7–9. See also Robin Schuldenfrei, 'Introduction to "Questions of Fashion",' *West 86th* 21, no. 1 (2014): 102–20.
2 _____ Reich, 'Modefragen,' 7–9.
3 _____ Lilly Reich, 'Die Ausstellung "Kunsthandwerk in der Mode",' *Mitteilungen des Verbandes der deutschen Mode-Industrie* 10 (1919): 208–11.
4 _____ Reich, 'Die Ausstellung "Kunsthandwerk in der Mode",' 209.
5 _____ Reich, 210–211.
6 _____ Reich, 211.
7 _____ Frederic J. Schwartz, *The Werkbund* (New Haven: Yale University Press, 1996), 26–27.
8 _____ Schwartz, *The Werkbund*.
9 _____ Reich, 'Modefragen,' 8.
10 _____ Reich, 'Modefragen'.
11 _____ On exhibition designs, see Matilda McQuaid, 'Lilly Reich and the Art of Exhibition Design,' in *Lilly Reich: designer and architect (New York: Museum of Modern Art, 1996):* 9–45 and Wallis Miller, 'Mies and Exhibitions,' in Terence Riley and Barry Bergdoll, eds., *Mies in Berlin*, exh. cat. (New York: The Museum of Modern Art, 2001): 338–349.
12 _____ See Robin Schuldenfrei, *Luxury and Modernism: Architecture and the Object in Germany 1900-1933* (Princeton: Princeton University Press, 2018).
13 _____ Contract between Mies van der Rohe and Thonet-Mundus AG Zurich, 1931, Mies Archive, The Museum of Modern Art.
14 _____ *Mies van der Rohe: Architecture and Design in Stuttgart, Barcelona, Brno*, eds. Alexander von Vegesack and Matthias Kries et al., exh. cat. (Vienna: Vitra Design Museum & Skira, 1998), 44.
15 _____ Christiane Lange, *Mies van der Rohe and Lilly Reich: Furniture and Interiors* (Ostfildern: Hatje Cantz, 2006), 107; 156–159.
16 _____ Grete Tugendhat, 'On the Construction of the Tugendhat House,' in Daniela Hammer-Tugendhat, Ivo Hammer and Wolf Tegethoff (eds.), *Tugendhat House. Ludwig Mies van der Rohe* (Basel-Berlin: Birkhäuser-De Gruyter, 2020): 21.
17 _____ Philip Johnson, *Mies van der Rohe* (New York: The Museum of Modern Art, 1947), 60.
18 _____ See Marianne Eggler, 'Divide and Conquer: Ludwig Mies van der Rohe and Lilly Reich's Fabric Partitions at the Tugendhat House,' *Studies in the Decorative Arts* 16, no. 2 (2009): 66–90; Enrique Colomés and Gonzalo Moure, *Mies van der Rohe Café de Terciopelo y Seda Berlín, 27* (Madrid: Ed. Rueda, 2004).
19 _____ See General Office File, Patents, Lorenz and Reich, 1937–1940, boxes 47 and 48, Mies Archive, Library of Congress.

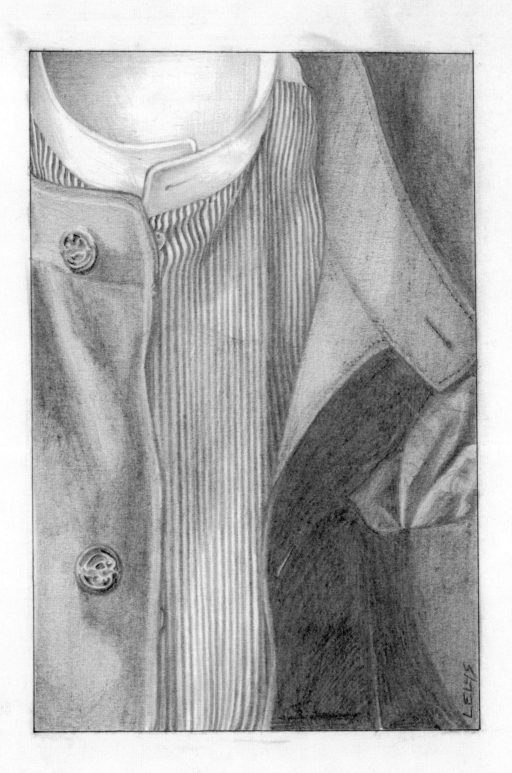

THE PHANTOM JACKET: LE CORBUSIER AND THE OBSCURE LEGACY OF THE FORESTIÈRE

Ian Erickson

The persona of the architect first emerged in the Renaissance, when the discipline elevated itself above the building trades, professionalising what was previously a vocational pursuit. This schism created the need for a distinct professional identity, as, like doctors and priests, architects now required a uniform. Michelangelo was arguably the first to mould the discipline's sartorial culture with his all-black clothing immortalised in Domenico Cresti's painting *Michelangelo Presenting the Model for the Completion of St Peter's to Pope Pius IV* from 1619 (Fig. 3). Michelangelo's black vestments embody the newfound anxieties of the client-patron profession, in which architects needed to brand themselves in order to attract commissions that, once won, defined the architect – no matter their external status or personal success – as someone subservient to a client. The quasi-clerical black robes of Michelangelo are thus self-consciously reflective of those of his client, Pope Pius IV, while simultaneously projecting blankness, severity, and humility.[1] Some four hundred years later, Frank Gehry, arguably the most famous contemporary architect, took a similar approach of sartorial mirroring when presenting his model of the Facebook headquarters to Mark Zuckerberg while wearing a black version of Zuckerberg's uniform of a plain T-shirt.[2]

All-black clothing is now ubiquitous within the discipline of architecture, and its diverse associations with other social groups, such as punks, beatniks, and monks, are all useful in cultivating the architect's mystique.[3] Yet, despite these varied associations, architects' singular disciplinary uniform makes them unique among the creative professions. Artists have a far greater diversity of personas – Hockney's irreverent prep, Basquiat's dressed-down Armani – while the paucity of architects dressing outside the dominant mode highlights the profession's curious and self-conscious tendency towards similarity. Despite this uniformity, architects are tellingly sensitive about their shared preference, with figures like Rem Koolhaas (falsely) claiming, 'I never wear black!'[4] This refusal to acknowledge the architect's sartorial persona exposes an anxiety central to the field, with architects simultaneously exerting high levels of control over their clothing while sidestepping critical discussions of dress.

No other figure is a better exemplar of this tendency than the late Charles-Édouard Jeanneret (1887-1965), better known by his nom de plume Le Corbusier, who skilfully constructed his public persona through fashion and dress. As Beatriz Colomina argues in *Publicity and Privacy*, modernity marked the 'publicity of the private' through image culture, with Modernist figures like Le Corbusier disseminating highly composed images of both their architecture and themselves through photographs, films, exhibitions, and advertisements.[5] Indeed, Le Corbusier's highly publicised appearance still affects perceptions of the profession today, and to many, the architect is still a white man in a dark suit (Fig. 2) and circular glasses.

Le Corbusier's careful control over his clothing is epitomised by the curious history of the Forestière (*forestier*: French for a person who works in a forest), a jacket the architect supposedly commissioned from the Parisian boutique Arnys in 1947 at the age of 60 as a custom garment to draw in. Being the only item of clothing the iconic modernist architect commissioned for such

1 Lelys for Arnys, drawing of the collar of the Forestière, Dominique Lelys.

use, the Forestière should be a canonical garment, central to Le Corbusier's legacy and persona, yet it is little known both within and outside architectural circles, and there is no substantive reference to or documentation of its existence within the literature native to the discipline nor even within the archive of Le Corbusier himself.[6] The Forestière's fringe history of suppression and reproduction provides an object lesson in the power of clothing, both in its material presence and in its intentional obscurity.

Former Arnys proprietor Jean Grimbert claims his father Léon cut the pattern for the Forestière based on Le Corbusier's precise specifications. The body of the jacket was modelled after a classic Sologne gamekeeper's jacket[7] famously worn by Gaston Modot in the celebrated 1939 French film *La Règle du Jeu* (*The Rules of The Game*) (Fig. 4). While the body of the jacket was structured, militaristic and French, the sleeves took on a distinctly different character, being based on those of a kimono, with a wide consistent width from armhole to cuff allowing for unrestricted movement.[8] The wide sleeve provided the architect-designer-painter-sculptor the ability to, quite literally, 'roll up his sleeves and get his hands dirty'. Like the sleeves, the collar might also be Asian-inspired, substituting the pointed flap collar of the French gamekeeper's jacket for a standing mandarin collar whose origins trace back to the Ming Dynasty in China (1368-1644) where it was worn on both men's and women's garments. Today, this mandarin collar is more popularly known as a 'Nehru collar' after its popularization by Jawaharlal Nehru, Prime Minister of India from 1947 to 1964, whom Le Corbusier met with on multiple occasions while the architect was working on the Chandigarh Master Plan project.[9]

With its clothing components from different cultures, the Forestière allowed the garment to overcome the particular shortcomings of the original gamekeeper's jacket and of all menswear tailored in the French tradition, whose tapered sleeves and structured shoulders are ideal for cutting a heroic figure but not well suited to the dexterous labour of drawing. The Forestière's sleeve heads were pivoted slightly off-centre to provide ergonomic specificity for the act of drawing, structurally reinforcing the jacket's definition as a tool.[10] In the material articulation of this 'workwear' commission, Le Corbusier subscribed to the architect's penchant for black clothing and had the jacket made up in a colourway fit for his adopted moniker of 'the crow-like one': black wide-wale corduroy with black silk lining.[11]

Arnys introduced the Forestière into their ready-to-wear line in the 1950s, and the jacket immediately became synonymous with the brand. These commercial reproductions were quite different from the original commission as the black corduroy was substituted for linens, cashmeres and leathers in all the colours of the rainbow, while the silk lining was often rendered in contrasting hues and patterns. In the 1980s, there were more structural changes, with Jean Grimbert and director of style Dominique Lelys modifying the Forestière by removing its structuring and padding. This version was so popular that 'it became the best-seller for Arnys, accounting for 50% of their sales'.[12]

Given the long and surely incomplete history of changes and reproductions, the exact details of the original seem impossible to pin down.[13] While a photograph of Le Corbusier wearing the jacket would help sort out

these differences, none exist. This absence is most apparent when such photographs can't be found in Arnys's own advertisements. Arnys built itself into an institution that counted the likes of Yves Saint Laurent, Jean-Paul Sartre and François Mitterrand among its loyal clientele, in part by crafting its brand identity around Le Corbusier and the Forestière's mystique. As the menswear historian and tailor Alan Flusser wrote in his review of the boutique in 1996, 'Arnys was for the bohemian dandy or boulevardier – such as the late Gide, Cocteau, Le Corbusier, and even the rough-hewn Hemingway.'[14] It is noteworthy that Flusser doesn't even refer to the Forestière by name in the review, instead calling it the 'Corbusier jacket'. Given the effort put into linking Arnys, Le Corbusier and the Forestière, one can be reasonably sure that if any such image existed, it would be used by Arnys in their advertisements.

The absence of any photographs of the original Forestière could be attributed to Le Corbusier's meticulous control over his public image, achieved through the curation of his own archive, the Paris-based Fondation Le Corbusier, which was established by the architect himself in 1960, granting him preternatural control over his legacy. The architect preserved, assembled and edited the archive's collection to extend his control over his public image past his natural life. He is reported to have 'obsessively preserved every letter, drawing, and photograph for posterity', with each addition or omission being the result of Le Corbusier's own curatorial decisions.[15] As Beatriz Colomina argues, Le Corbusier hides among this abundance of traces a mountain of archival excess where absence is more significant than presence.[16] While the lack of photographs from the archive is indeed telling, so too is the absence of the garment itself. Instead, the only sartorial objects Le Corbusier deemed worthy of preservation are now housed within a category titled 'glasses and ocular instruments Z1-10', a collection of the many pairs of identical iconic glasses he owned. Le Corbusier thus symbolically elevates the discrimination of his eyes above the labours of his hands, whose movement the Forestière was commissioned to better facilitate, betraying an aversion to exposing both his act of working and the garments he worked in. This is symptomatic of the way Le Corbusier represented (or misrepresented) his process of drawing, famously disingenuously simulating the act during the fourth CIAM (Congrès Internationaux d'Architecture Moderne) meeting in 1933 by briskly tracing over lightly projected drawings he had prepared beforehand – all while wearing the very sort of restrictive suit that inspired the Forestière in the first place.[17] Or, in the famous photograph of Le Corbusier nude painting Eileen Gray's *E1027*, a representation of labour where he is not actually 'at work', as the mural is already finished – as if, like Athena springing forth from a gash in Zeus's head, the mural was born complete, straight from the mind of its father.[18]

Both of these public drawing spectacles by Le Corbusier carry gendered and racialised histories, highlighting the role of drawing as a potent form of cultural and material inscription. The Forestière, as a garment designed specifically to facilitate the act of drawing, therefore becomes implicated in the broader history of drawing as a fundamental human practice, connected to memory, technics and communication.[19] Indeed, the shift from pre-modern drawing to rule-based systems of perspective and

3 Domenico Cresti, *Michelangelo Presenting the Model for the Completion of St Peter's to Pope Pius IV*, oil on canvas, 1618-1619.

orthography marked the emergence of architecture as a formal discipline during the Renaissance, where architectural drawing co-evolved with the architect's identity and sartorial traditions. However, as John May has argued, today architects no longer draw. The adoption of digital tools has fundamentally altered our bodily relationship to design practice, with new technological frameworks replacing 'drawing' as the architect's core activity.[20]

As such, the Forestière, a jacket designed to support the architect in the historical act of drawing, is a product deeply rooted in its time and cultural context. Mid-twentieth-century architecture and design culture were heavily preoccupied with dressing the modern body, shaped by ideologies of gender, race and productivity. Architect Bernard Rudofsky's essay *Are Clothes Modern?*, published in 1947 – the same year Le Corbusier commissioned the Forestière – reflects this cultural moment. Rudofsky's MOMA exhibition of the same name questioned the cultural and social constructs shaping modern dress – in particular, the men's suit – situating it within longer histories of both Western and non-Western garments. Similarly, the modern architect Adolf Loos engaged with ideas of ornamentation, dress and Western masculinity in his writing, even giving material articulation to his ideologies when he designed the store for the renowned Viennese men's outfitter Knize in 1913.[21] In historicising this period in *White Walls, Designer Dresses: The Fashioning of Modern Architecture*, Mark Wigley connects the design of spaces to the design of bodies, arguing that the aesthetic principles of modernist architecture are closely tied to sartorial design.[22] Wigley emphasises the performative and symbolic dimensions of both architecture and fashion, showing how they collaboratively shape concepts of modernity and identity.

In this context, the curious absence of the Forestière from Le Corbusier's otherwise overabundant archive invites reflection on its significance as a cultural artefact. Does its obscurity suggest a deliberate omission in the carefully curated construction of his legacy and public persona? How might we unpack the garment's status as a fusion of Western and Asian sartorial traditions? What insights does it offer about modernity's connection to the bodily act of drawing? Within architecture's enduring interplay with fashion and clothing, the Forestière lingers as a spectral figure – an obscure yet manifest presence that exposes deep-seated disciplinary tensions intertwined with its history of marginalization.

3

4 Shooting *La Règle du jeu* (The Rules of the Game), 1939, photographed by Sam Levin, Médiathèque du Patrimoine et de la Photographie, Charenton-le-Pont.
5 Lelys for Arnys, watercolour of the Forestière, advertisement, Dominique Lelys.

Endnotes

1 _____ Other designers have notably adopted monks' robes as a kind of uniform, from the American architect and pioneer of 'Richardsonian Romanesque' Henry Hobson Richardson (1838-1868) to the Swiss Bauhaus master Johannes Itten (1888-1967).
2 _____ Frank Gehry presenting a model of the Facebook headquarters to Mark Zuckerberg. Adam Greenfield, 'Is Facebook's "Zee Town" more than just a Mark Zuckerberg vanity project?' *The Guardian* (10 March 2015), www.theguardian.com/cities/2015/mar/10/facebook-zee-town-mark-zuckerberg.
3 _____ For more on architectural culture and the colour black, see Mohsen Mostafavi and Max Raphael, *The Color Black: Antinomies of a Color in Architecture and Art* (London: Mack, 2024).
4 _____ Cornelia Rau, *Why Do Architects Wear Black?* (Vienna: Springer, 2008).
5 _____ Beatriz Colomina, *Privacy and Publicity* (Cambridge, MA: MIT Press, 1994).
6 _____ The author spoke with Antoine Picon, Chairman of Fondation Le Corbusier between 2013 and 2024, who confirmed that there is no material evidence of the Forestière in the archive nor any known photos of the garment being worn by the architect.
7 _____ www.parisiangentleman.com/blog/la-forestiere-symbole-de-lelegance-rive-gauche-depuis-1947.
8 _____ Le Corbusier has a long history with Japan, completing the National Museum of Western Art in Tokyo in 1959 and employing many Japanese Architects – Kunio Maekawa, Junzo Sakakura, and Takamasa Yoshizaka – in his Parisian studio. In his treatise '*Toward an Architecture*' (1923), Le Corbusier referred to the simplicity and functional beauty of Japanese craftsmanship and how it aligned with modern design ideals. However, some scholars, such as Reiner De Graff, Zeynep Çelik Alexander and Ken Tadashi Oshima, have critiqued Le Corbusier's admiration of Japan as 'orientalist', being a selective appreciation of a few 'exotic' features without full cultural context and in some cases reframing non-Western traditions to fit his own Western modernist paradigms.
9 _____ mitp-arch.mitpress.mit.edu/pub/55ayllas/release/1.
10 _____ www.parisiangentleman.com/blog/la-forestiere-symbole-de-lelegance-rive-gauche-depuis-1947.
11 _____ Le Corbusier literally translates to 'the crow-like one'.
12 _____ www.permanentstyle.com/2022/06/dominique-lelys-and-artumes-taking-on-the-spirit-of-arnys.html.
13 _____ Although there exists a design drawing of the original jacket, now part of the Berluti archives.
14 _____ Alan Flusser, *Style and the Man: How and Where to Buy the Best Men's Clothes* (New York: HarperCollins, 1996), 308.
15 _____ William J. R. Curtis, 'Le Corbusier: Ideas and Forms,' *ArchDaily* (April 10, 2015), www.archdaily.com/617466/le-corbusier-ideas-and-forms.
16 _____ Colomina, *Privacy and Publicity*.
17 _____ Malcolm Millais, *Le Corbusier: The Dishonest Architect* (Newcastle upon Tyne: Cambridge Scholars Publishing, 2017).
18 _____ This photograph has its own complex and gendered history; see Beatriz Colomina, 'Battle lines: E.1027,' *Renaissance and Modern Studies* 39, 1 (1996): 95–105, DOI: 10.1080/14735789609366597.
19 _____ Bernard Stiegler, *Technics and Time, 1: The Fault of Epimetheus*, trans. George Collins and Richard Beardsworth (Stanford, CA: Stanford University Press, 1998).
20 _____ John May, *Signal. Image. Architecture* (New York: Columbia Books on Architecture and the City, 2019).
21 _____ Adolf Loos, *Ornament and Crime: Selected Essays*, ed. Adolf Opel, trans. Michael Mitchell (Riverside, CA: Ariadne Press, 1998).
22 _____ Mark Wigley, *White Walls, Designer Dresses: The Fashioning of Modern Architecture* (Cambridge, MA: MIT Press, 1995).

La forestière

Un esprit de liberté, de non-conformisme, un style, un regard, un confort. L'élégance.

ARNYS

14, rue de Sèvres, Paris 7ᵉ

'This is a costume for a modern woman and no fashion creation: it has therefore a character more durable than ephemeral.'

'Ceci est un costume pour la femme d'aujourd'hui, et non pas une création de haute couture. Son caractère est donc permanent plutôt qu'éphémère.'
(Le Corbusier in a note to his clothing designs, 19 February 1952)

Le Corbusier, designs for women's clothes, published in *Formes et Vie*, 2, 1951, Fondation Le Corbusier, Paris. In February 1952, the architect sent a description of the clothes to the American fashion magazine *Harper's Bazaar*, asking them to publish his creations in the United States of America. He had the designs patented and emphasised the fact that they were not fashion creations but clothes in which women could move freely without losing their charm. He hoped they would be money-spinners, but the fashion magazine did not take him up on his request.

'The peasant loves ornament and decorates his walls. The civilized man wears a well-cut suit and is the owner of easel pictures and books.'

'Le paysan aime l'ornement et peint des fresques. Le civilisé porte le complet anglais et possède des tableaux de chevalet et des livres.' (Le Corbusier, *Vers une architecture*, 1925, 112, 115)

1   Front of Maison Guiette, where Ann Demeulemeester lived and worked for years, photographed by Victor Robyn, 2023.

ANN DEMEULEMEESTER, MARTIN MARGIELA, RAF SIMONS AND THE CROSS-POLLINATION OF FASHION AND INTERIORS

Romy Cockx

Over recent decades, numerous fashion houses have turned to the world of interiors to reinforce their brand identity, branching out with their own interior collections and design collabs, and opening luxury flagship stores to draw us in. In some cases, their vision of an interior is very much in keeping with their visual language and design methodology. Exponents of this are Belgian fashion designers Ann Demeulemeester, Martin Margiela and Raf Simons, who also prompt us to reflect on the historical relationship between fashion and interior.

LE CORBUSIER'S MAISON GUIETTE: THE PREDESTINATION OF THE PURIST COUPLE DEMEULEMEESTER-ROBYN

In 1983, fashion designer Ann Demeulemeester and photographer Patrick Robyn purchased Le Corbusier's one and only building in Belgium. The house cum studio had been built for the Antwerp painter René Guiette in 1926-1927. The young Robyn-Demeulemeester couple discovered the building in 1981 while looking for a location to photograph her modernist graduation collection. At the time, the building was being used by the contractor working on the nearby motorway. Although it was in a poor state of repair, they were smitten by the house and could not stop thinking about it.[1]

Captivated by its purist architecture, they moved in immediately after purchasing the building. However, damp problems forced them to vacate it temporarily.[2] In 1985, they appointed the architect Georges Baines to restore it, and the work was carried out in 1987-1988.[3] In 2017, Luc Deleu was commissioned to restore the building once again, and the work was completed in 2023. In 2016, Maison Guiette was added to the UNESCO World Heritage list, and the Robyn-Demeulemeester couple have now been the custodians of Le Corbusier's legacy for over forty years.

As a reaction to the mass destruction of the First World War and inspired by the production processes of the automobile industry, Le Corbusier developed pioneering concepts, which he crystalised in his Dom-Ino and Citrohan housing prototypes.[4] Maison Guiette gave him the opportunity to implement those concepts, albeit subject to urban-planning regulations and his client's wishes. The load-bearing side walls and the concrete skeleton support a free-plan view and the free design of the façades with horizontal windows. Le Corbusier also applied key principles from his Five Points of New Architecture in, for example, the roof terrace, while the cellar windows are a subtle reference to his *pilotis* or pillars.[5]

At Maison Guiette, Le Corbusier also put into practice his evolving ideas about the use of colour, drawing on his expertise as a painter. He insisted on deciding on the colours on site after completion of the building[6] on the grounds that colours sculpture a space.[7] He combined natural pigments such as ochre, sienna and ultramarine with white, taking into account their psychological effect and the natural light.[8]

The house made a deep and lasting impression on Demeulemeester: 'This house has always meant a great deal for my work. The purity of the building has helped me in my collections.'[9] In particular, Le Corbusier's purist ideals resonated in her 1996 Spring-Summer collection (Fig. 8), which she described as a watershed: 'I reached a crucial point with the summer collection. The silhouettes are consistently clean and pure. I ruled out anything that smacked of decoration. I had never gone that far.'[10] In the early 1920s, Le Corbusier published his aesthetic theory of purism, which advocated a methodical refinement of form.[11] A comparison can be drawn between his approach to architecture as 'pure création de l'esprit' and Demeulemeester's approach

GUIETTE
Anvers

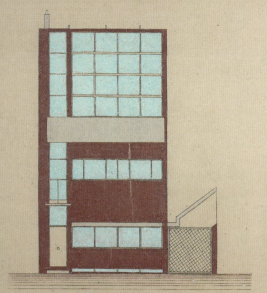

FAÇADE SUR RUE

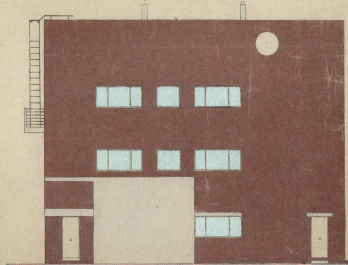

FAÇADE LATÉRALE

2

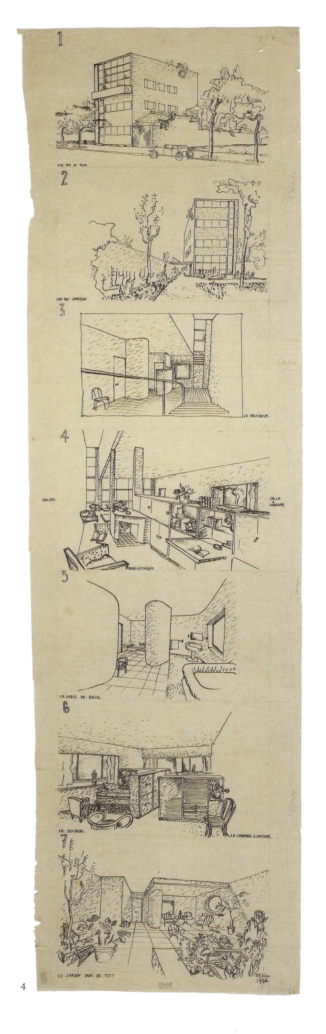

4

2   Le Corbusier, design drawing for Maison Guiette, 10 March 1926, Fondation Le Corbusier, Paris.
3   Maquette of Maison Guiette, c. 1987, Flemish Architecture Institute – Flemish Community collection, Georges Baines archive, Antwerp.
4   Le Corbusier, sketches of Maison Guiette, Fondation Le Corbusier, Paris.

'In this house, I learned about light, proportions and respect for pure lines.'[12]

(Ann Demeulemeester)

Ann Demeulemeester in the third-floor office of the Le Corbusier house

5 Living room at Maison Guiette, photographed by Victor Robyn, 2024.
6 Ann Demeulemeester in the atelier at Maison Guiette, photographed by Jean-Philippe Piter for *W Fashion Feature*, June 1995.
7 Stairwell at Maison Guiette, photographed by Victor Robyn, 2024.
8 Ann Demeulemeester, sleeveless open-back top with trousers, Spring-Summer 1996, MoMu, Antwerp, X1409.

9 Ann Demeulemeester for Serax, porcelain plates featuring dégradé edges painted by hand from the *Dé* series, and feather, 2018.
10 Ann Demeulemeester, asymmetric blazer and shirt over a roll-neck jumper and trousers, Autumn-Winter 1996-1997, MoMu, Antwerp, X1408.

11 Atelier on the third floor of Maison Guiette, photographed by Victor Robyn, 2024.
12 Ground floor of Ann Demeulemeester's flagship store in Antwerp, photographed by Victor Robyn, 2021.
13 First floor of Ann Demeulemeester's flagship store in Antwerp, photographed by Victor Robyn, 2021.

to fashion. She always likes to start from scratch, in search of the ultimate exactness of a form inspired by emotion and desire.

Her use of colour also revolves around precision and poetry: 'For me black and white signify simplicity and essence. It is rather like looking at a black and white film. Without colour, you can feel and see everything. I concentrate on the architectural and do not want to be distracted by colours and patterns. For me black is the most poetic colour, the strongest too. White is the light, the purest. Every now and then I fancy working with colours, but I approach them as shades, like the play of light and shadow.'[13]

In 1996, when the Belgian furniture manufacturer Bulo gave Demeulemeester carte blanche to design a piece of furniture, she presented a simple table covered in white artist's canvas tacked down with rivets (Fig. 15). Underneath the table is the label with which she also signs her fashion collections. Patrick Robyn and Ann Demeulemeester's *Table Blanche* referenced the archetype of a table that bears all the marks of time. The virginal white canvas has a special meaning for them. They also overlaid it with invitations to her fashion shows and the catwalk itself. Moreover, canvas plays an important role in the interior of Ann Demeulemeester's flagship store on Leopold de Waelplaats in Antwerp, where wall panels covered with artist's canvas envelop it like a second skin and filter the incoming daylight. This nineteenth-century corner building was renovated by architect Paul Robbrecht in collaboration with Patrick Robyn in 1999. The historic façade was restored, but the inside of the building was stripped to evoke Demeulemeester's atelier space. Painted white, the metal columns that were revealed when the internal walls were removed refer to Le Corbusier's *pilotis*. The interplay of lines in the interior resonates with Maison Guiette's artistic idiom and provides the ideal setting for Demeulemeester's garments, furniture, lighting and homeware.[14] Fashion and interior design, work and private life, function and emotion converge here in the Robyn-Demeulemeester couple's purist Gesamtkunstwerk.

14 Ann Demeulemeester, invitation for fashion show overlaid with canvas, Spring-Summer 1996, MoMu, Antwerp, B18/1.
15 Ann Demeulemeester and Patrick Robyn for Bulo, Table Blanche, canvas over wood, 1996, photographed by Patrick Robyn.

MAISON MARTIN MARGIELA'S WHITE LAYERING

Martin Margiela is regarded as the last designer to bring about a revolution in fashion. When he founded Maison Martin Margiela with Jenny Meirens in 1988, he chose white as the base colour. The brightest of all colours served to connect every element of the fashion house: 'To present the extreme fashion I had in mind, I thought it was very important to show it in a kind of universe. It had to be constructed around a colour. In the late 1980s, most of the showrooms and shops would be grey concrete with black design furniture. And I started thinking: how to be different? So I came up with a different colour. And that colour would be white. Since there was no budget at the start, I would find junk furniture in the street or at the Salvation Army. When it had an interesting design, it would be painted; otherwise, it was covered in white cotton.'[15]

Margiela may have been inspired by his mother, who enjoyed repurposing second-hand furniture,[16] but as Chris Dercon remarked, his 'whitewash' also calls to mind Le Corbusier.[17] In 1925, the modernist architect posited 'La loi du Ripolin – The Law of Ripolin'[18] – as a revolutionary substance.[19] All ornamentation could be banished with whitewash and the result would be purity and moral cleansing: 'Imagine the effect of the Law of Ripolin. Every citizen has to replace his drapes, his damasks, his wallpaper and his stencils with a plain coat of white Ripolin. The home is made clean. There are no more dirty or dark corners. *Everything is shown as it is.*'[20] Illustrated by two advertisements for Hermès leather goods, he criticised decorated clutter: 'a luxury object is well made, neat and clean, pure and wholesome, and its bareness reveals the quality of its manufacture'. He could still tolerate a fashionable young woman in a floral dress, but he found the ubiquity of ornamentation repugnant. In his opinion, the midinette looked best in

16 The atelier of the Maison Margiela showroom, 1991, photographed by Marina Faust.
17 Four vintage armchairs dressed in a single white linen cover in Maison Martin Margiela's shop, 25 bis rue de Montpensier in Paris, c. 2002.

'To present the extreme fashion I had in mind, I thought it was very important to show it in a kind of universe. It had to be constructed around a colour.'

(Martin Margiela)

'a pretty, bright, clear room, white walls, good cane chair or the Thonet; table from the bazar de l'Hôtel-de-Ville (department store) (Louis-XIII tradition, very nice table) painted with Ripolin'.[21]

Maison Martin Margiela unconsciously translated the Law of Ripolin for the postmodern era. Like Le Corbusier, the fashion house associated white with honesty and purity, but also with fragility and transience. The 'clutter' was not discarded, but given a white coat. Vintage furniture, crystal chandeliers, strip lighting, telephones, radios, air-conditioning, box files and office supplies: white froze everything into a moment in time and brought past time into focus. 'White means the strength of fragility and the fragility of the passage of time. An expression of unity, purity and honesty. It is never just white but more – whites – all the shades possible! We usually use matt white so that the passage of time is evident.'[22] The layer of white was used not only for the inside of the offices, ateliers, showrooms and shops, but also on clothing and accessories. The paint crackles as it is worn, gradually revealing the colour and texture of the underlying item. So the painted object acts as a palimpsest, slowly divulging a hidden past.[23]

Margiela also underlined the transient nature of fashion and interiors with trompe l'oeils. The fashion house moved to several different addresses within Paris but took its history with it by integrating into the new premises photographs of elements from the interiors of previous locations. From 2004 to 2023, the offices were located in a nineteenth-century building which had originally served as a charitable institution and from 1939 housed a school for industrial design. Maison Martin Margiela covered the original furniture with a layer of white paint and created a surrealist labyrinth by plastering the existing doors with photocopies of other doors and adding extra door panels and white ladders that led nowhere. The front door of the apartment on Boulevard Saint Denis, where the showroom was initially situated, reappeared, and black and white photographs of a whole range of interior features evoked the atmosphere of the eighteenth-century *hôtel particulier* – private mansion – on Rue Faubourg Poissonnière, where the offices were located between 2000 and 2004. The baroque mirrors, marble mantelpieces, ornamental frames and rosettes were also produced photographically in various Margiela shops all over the world (Fig. 22).[24] Just as the (white-painted) Stockman dressmaker dummies and the white coats worn by the staff were a nod to the history of French couture, the historical interior features recalled the decors of couture salons like Worth, Doucet and Paquin with their Louis XVI furnishings.

Margiela applied the same layering to garments by screen-printing onto them black-and-white photographs of vintage items of clothing (Spring-Summer 1996). In the 2004-2005 Autumn-Winter collection, interior and fashion literally flowed over into each other in trompe l'oeil Chesterfield prints (Fig. 21). The interplay between fashion and interior was also expressed in the fashion house's transformation and deconstruction methods. For the 2006-2007 Autumn-Winter collection, Margiela disassembled sofas waiting to be upholstered in white fabric. He removed the leather upholstery from the seat, draped it over a dummy and made it into a jacket (Fig. 19, p. 54).[25] The instinctive desire to dismantle constructions and reuse materials to arrive at something surprisingly new is expressed in all that Martin Margiela touches.

18

18 Maison Martin Margiela, hand-painted vintage handbag encased in a made-to-measure white-cotton cover, Autumn-Winter 2002-2003, MoMu, Antwerp, B05/1.
19 Maison Martin Margiela, pair of Tabi ankle boots in black leather painted white, c. 1990, MoMu, Antwerp, B13/25ab.
20 The ceiling of the Maison Martin Margiela showroom, 1991, photographed by Ronald Stoops.
21 Maison Martin Margiela, leather jacket with trompe l'œil Chesterfield print, Autumn-Winter 2004-2005, MoMu, Antwerp, T24/269.

19

22 Interior of the Maison Martin Margiela shop in Los Angeles, with trompe l'œil photograph of the interior of the previous office on rue Faubourg Poissonnière, c. 2008.
23 Maison Martin Margiela, white-painted vintage gilet, wool, Spring-Summer 2004, MoMu, Antwerp, T18/655.

CORPO AND QUILTS: RAF SIMONS'S PROTECTIVE WRAPPINGS

Raf Simons, one of the most influential fashion designers of the last twenty-five years, has no formal education in fashion, having studied industrial design at the Higher Institute for Visual Communication and Design (Stedelijk Hoger Instituut voor Visuele Kommunikatie en Vormgeving) in Genk.[26] In 1989, his interest in fashion led to an internship with fashion designer Walter Van Beirendonck, who took him to Paris Fashion Week (Spring-Summer 1990), where Simons attended the shows of Jean Paul Gaultier and Maison Martin Margiela. His compatriot's iconic 'white show' left an indelible impression on him: 'Nothing else in fashion has had such a big impact on me. Only at that point did I understand what fashion could be or what it could mean to people.'[27]

In June 1991, Simons graduated with *Corpo*, a collection dedicated to linking fashion design and furniture design. He used seven 'accessory cabinets' to convey the central idea of the relationship between the human body on the inside and the outside structure of the product. All the pieces have a basic cylindrical form on four legs that is enclosed or clad in different materials such as leather, textile, wire mesh or Niroflex. Simons described his design method as follows: 'The way I work consists of collecting everything I think might be interesting to reimagine as a new product: ideas, materials, drawings, theories of forms, texts, products, images, photographs, video, film, visions, information, philosophies and so on. [...] The challenge is to bring different elements from the collection together in a harmonious manner in a single design, in other words: turn disorder into order.'[28] In an accompanying signed VHS video cassette, a woman's voice coupled with a monotonous droning soundtrack explains the concept: each product can be seen as a body, with an inside and an outside. Derived from different cultures and periods, Simons's visual sources reveal a universal human desire to protect, decorate and transform the body. From a gender perspective, it is interesting that he links 'male' with functionality by means of a leather casing with multiple pockets on the inside that can be turned into a toilet bag (Figs. 29 & 30). The obsession with the perfect, artificial female body was expressed in a lace-up corset with a metal back support (Figs. 25 & 27). This type of garment was the focus of the Gaultier show that Simons attended. In his 1990 Spring-Summer collection, Margiela, who was Gaultier's assistant from 1984 to 1987, also referred to the way clothes shape the body. He drew attention to the connection between the inside and the outside, which intrigued Simons, by outlining the seams of clear plastic jackets with white bias tape.

Corpo was favourably received and shown in several galleries,[29] but Simons dreamed of fashion.[30] He was now represented by Linda Loppa, head of the fashion department at the Royal Academy of Fine Arts (Koninklijke Academie voor Schone Kunsten) in Antwerp, who urged him to learn tailoring under her father Renzo Loppa. In 1995, Simons launched his fashion label retaining the typography with which he signed his furniture. His design methodology also remained unchanged: the collections he designed under his own name, but later also for fashion houses like Jil Sander, Dior, Calvin Klein and Prada, were developed from a rich and varied seedbed. Simons sees fashion as a way of exploring society, in collaboration with others.[31]

In particular, this approach was expressed in his vision for the American clothing brand Calvin Klein. For the 2017-2018 Autumn-Winter collection, Simons turned vintage quilts, collected from all over America, into coats and parka linings. In the 2018 Spring-Summer collection, patchwork quilts played a prominent role.[32] Quilting is the age-old technique of stitching together layers of fabric to form a thick padding. In the case of a patchwork quilt, the top layer consists of scraps of different coloured fabric sewn together according to a specific design. They are used as bedspreads or wall coverings and played an important role in American culture as an art form (especially female) and as social glue.[33] Quilted plaid made a further appearance in Simons's 2018-2019 Autumn-Winter collection, but this time with a backing of Mylar, a thermal material used for (among other things) emergency blankets. Dressed in matching chiffon patchwork dresses, the models wore the plaids draped nonchalantly over their forearm. The historical symbolism of the patchwork patterns was connection ('Irish Chain') and hospitality ('Pineapple'), but also slavery ('Bear Paw'). The 'Log Cabin Quilt' (Fig. 35) references the beam structure of the houses of the American pioneers and symbolises home, warmth, love and safety.[34]

Simons also linked the two Calvin Klein collections to a familiar beacon from the desolate American landscape: the wooden prairie barn. It provided the setting for the 2018 Spring-Summer campaign, the interior furnished with patchwork quilts (Fig. 32), and for the 2018-2019 Autumn-Winter runway show. Here three barns reconstructed from reclaimed wood dated to the nineteenth century papered with photo prints of artworks by Andy Warhol stood amid deep drifts of popcorn. Simons combined heroic firefighter-style jackets with long prairie dresses, bala-clavas and Looney Tunes references into his vision of the American dream (Fig. 36). That the dream sometimes turns into a nightmare is clear from Todd Haynes's film *Safe* (1995), an important inspiration for Simons. The psychological thriller makes the paranoia of a privileged Californian housewife alarmingly tangible. Suffering from a succession of symptoms seemingly caused by toxic environmental factors, she eventually withdraws from society.

24 Raf Simons, *Corpo* graduation collection, FLTR: accessory cabinets 'Butcher', 'Corset', 'Snake', 'Male Accessory', 'Burma', 'Wire Netting' and 'Chain', 1991.

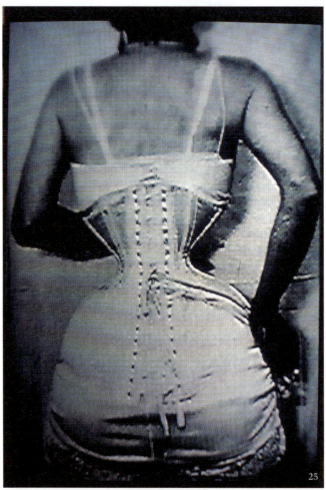

25 Inspiration image for the 'Corset' accessory cabinet from the *Corpo* video, Raf Simons graduation collection, 1991.
26 Raf Simons, detail of the 'Butcher' accessory cabinet, *Corpo* graduation collection, 1991.
27 Raf Simons, 'Corset' accessory cabinet, *Corpo* graduation collection, 1991.
28 Raf Simons, 'Wire Netting' accessory cabinet, *Corpo* graduation collection, 1991.
29 Raf Simons, 'Male Accessory' accessory cabinet, *Corpo* graduation collection, 1991.
30 Raf Simons, part of an accessory cabinet, 'Male Accessory', *Corpo* graduation collection, 1991.

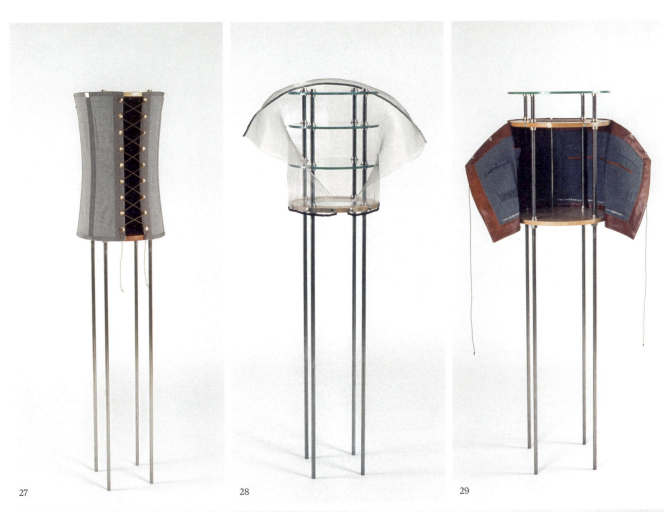

27

28

29

30

31 Raf Simons for Calvin Klein and Cassina, *Feltri* series of chairs covered with patchwork quilts, presented at Design Miami/Basel, June 2018.

32 Raf Simons for Calvin Klein 20539NYC, campaign photographed by Willy Vanderperre, Spring-Summer 2018.

'What we must never forget when designing for the interior is the sense of hominess.'[36]

(Raf Simons)

The wooden barn resurfaced at Design/Miami Basel (June 2018), where, partnered with Cassina, Simons presented his interpretation of the iconic Feltri armchair, designed by Gaetano Pesce in 1987. Simons replaced the plain quilted upholstery of the original design with one-of-a-kind 'heirloom' patchwork quilts 'emblematic of both American heritage and a homespun, handcrafted ethos of days gone by'.[35] The flexible backrest of the felt throne lends itself to hugging the body. Simons contrasted this protective seat with a less comfortable chair: printed onto the wooden barn was Andy Warhol's *Electric Chair* from 1964 (Fig. 31).

The furniture and collections discussed here display a profound awareness of human vulnerability and a hankering for protection, hominess and comfort. Simons also mentions this when talking about his favourite furniture designers: he does not like the cold interiors of the 1980s, much preferring the mid-century designs of George Nakashima, Jean Prouvé, Jean Royère, Le Corbusier, Pierre Jeanneret and Charlotte Perriand, which he associates with human warmth and social responsibility. During his spell at Jil Sander, he reflected on the day-to-day lives of women when not in the company of men. For him, a picture of a model taking a nap on a rug in the living room of Charles and Ray Eames, which was published in an article in *Vogue* in 1954 (Fig. 33), represents 'a domesticity that doesn't feel contrived. These pictures aren't about fashion, they are about life'.[37]

33 The interior of Charles and Ray Eames's house in the Pacific Palisades neighbourhood of LA, photographed by Karen Radkai, 'California Ideas', *Vogue*, 15 April 1954.

Endnotes

1 _____ Conversation between Patrick Robyn, Ann Demeulemeester and Romy Cockx on August 19, 2024.
2 _____ Demeulemeester was pregnant at the time, and social services Kind & Gezin deemed the house unsuitable for a new-born baby.
3 _____ Among other things, Baines replaced the natural slates, which had been attached to the outer walls at the end of WWII, with white render as per Le Corbusier's initial design sketches. In 1993-95, he designed and also realised the adjoining atelier, which housed the Ann Demeulemeester fashion house until 2020.
4 _____ William JR Curtis, *Le Corbusier: Ideas and Forms* (London: Phaidon, 2015), 75, 100.
5 _____ Rudy De Graef, 'Le Corbusiers huis Guiette, de restauratie van een ruimtelijk gedicht,' *M&L* 43, 2 (2024), 55.
6 _____ Georges Baines and Els Spitaels, *Le Corbusier te Antwerpen. De woning Guiette* (Antwerp: Hoger Architectuurinstituut van het rijk (now Hogeschool Antwerpen), 1987), 70.
7 _____ 'La colour pouvait nous apporter l'espace' in Le Corbusier, 'Pessac,' *L'Architecture vivante* 17 (1927): 30.
8 _____ According to Le Corbusier, white makes for a lucid mind and is supported by the stimulating power of colour. Red requires bright light if it is to come into its own, while blue requires an umbra light. See Mark Wigley, *White Walls, Designer Dresses: The Fashioning of Modern Architecture* (Cambridge: The MIT Press, 1995), 215.
9 _____ Lut Clincke, *Vrouwenmode* (September 2007).
10 _____ *Mode dit is Belgisch* (13 March 1996).
11 _____ On the one hand, in the magazine *l'Esprit Nouveau*, which he published with Ozenfant, and later in *Vers une Architecture* (1923).
12 _____ Thomas Brown, 'A Lesson in Design with Ann Demeulemeester,' www.brownthomas.com/magazine/issue-14/lesson-in-design-ann-demeulemeester.html, accessed on December 13, 2024.
13 _____ *Catchy* 31 (2007).
14 _____ Demeulemeester has been collaborating with Serax to produce porcelain, cutlery and glassware since 2019. In 2022, they also launched a furniture collection.
15 _____ Martin Margiela in Rainer Holzemer, *Martin Margiela: In His Own Words*, documentary, 2019, 10min09-10min38.
16 _____ Geert Bruloot refers to this in: Alison Chernick, *Martin Margiela: That Artist Is Absent*, documentary, 2015.
17 _____ Chris Dercon, 'Mode als de verborgen zijde van de maan: Maan Ray,' in Martin Margiela, *Maison Martin Margiela* (New York: Rizzoli, 2009).
18 _____ Ripolin is a French manufacturer of weather-resistant enamel paint. The trade name became a verb: 'ripoliner'.
19 _____ Architectural historian Mark Wigley described the white wall of modernist architecture as 'the antifashion look' in Mark Wigley, *White Walls, Designer Dress. The Fashioning of Modern Architecture* and recently placed Le Corbusier's call for whiteness in a context of racialisation and disease: www.e-flux.com/architecture/sick-architecture/360099/chronic-whiteness/.
20 _____ 'Concevez les effets de la Loi du Ripolin. Chaque citoyen est tenu de remplacer ses tentures, ses damas, ses papiers peints, ses pochoirs, par une couche pure de ripolin blanc. On fait propre *chez soi* : il n'y a plus nulle part de coin sale, ni de coin sombre : *tout se montre comme ça est*,' Le Corbusier, *L'Art décoratif d'aujourd'hui* (Paris: Les éditions G. Crès, 1925), 191.
21 _____ '[L']objet de luxe est bien fait, net et propre, pur et sain, et sa nudité en révèle la bienfacture' and 'une gentile chambre claire et limpide, mur blanc, bonne chaise de paille ou de Thonet ; table du bazar de l'Hôtel-de-Ville (tradition Louis XIII, très belle table) peinte au ripolin', Le Corbusier, 90–91.
22 _____ 'Maison Martin Margiela' in *Cream*, Maison Martin Margiela special issue, No. 9 (2008): 124.
23 _____ Kaat Debo, *Maison Martin Margiela '20' The Exhibition* (Antwerp: MoMu, 2008), 11.
24 _____ Debo, *Maison Martin Margiela*, 4.
25 _____ See also Romy Cockx' contribution in this book: 'Wearing the Home in Times of Trouble', 40 et seq.
26 _____ Since 2012 known as the LUCA School of Arts.
27 _____ Raf Simons in 2016, published online: www.dazeddigital.com/fashion/article/38619/1/raf-simons-according-to-raf-simons-best-quotes-history.
28 _____ Raf Simons, 'Accessoiremeubel,' in *Eindexamen. Industriële vormgeving* (Genk: Higher Institute for Visual Communication and Design - Stedelijk Hoger Instituut voor Visuele Kommunikatie en Vormgeving, 1991), 13.
29 _____ Ziggurat in Ghent and IOTA in Antwerp, see Moniek E. Bucquoye, 'Een kastje met een jasje,' *Knack Weekend* (January 29, 1992): 42–45 and 'Kasten als mensen,' *De Morgen* (January 11, 1992): 58.
30 _____ Although in 1993 he also produced the 'Agena 1' and 'Black Hole' seats.
31 _____ 'When I was studying industrial and furniture design in Genk, it felt very much like me on my own. The reason I decided against it was because I thought it would be so nice to be in this kind of social environment, to always have a dialogue with people and a constant collaboration. In that way, fashion felt very alive.' Raf Simons in conversation with Tim Blanks, *Interview Magazine* (February 21, 2014).
32 _____ Lili Göksenin, 'Raf's Vintage Quilts at Calvin Klein Are Covetable, Political Fashion at Its Very Best,' *GQ Style* (September 19, 2017), www.gq.com/story/raf-simons-covetable-vintage-quilts-at-calvin-klein
33 _____ Maud Thiery, *Quilts: Een traditionele Amerikaanse volkskunst* (Gent: Maud Thiery, 1986), 6.
34 _____ Thiery, 12.
35 _____ www.instagram.com/cassinaofficial/p/Bj-OmMlnWL-/.
36 _____ Raf Simons on his collaboration with Kvadrat: *Knack Weekend* (December 18, 2014), weekend.knack.be/lifestyle/design/6-vragen-aan-raf-simons-over-zijn-stoffenontwerpen-voor-kvadrat/.
37 _____ Raf Simons in conversation with Mark Holgate, 'Nostalgia,' *Vogue US*,' (2012).

With thanks to Ann Demeulemeester, Patrick Robyn, Victor Robyn, Martin Margiela, Yaël Coopman, Casimir and Max Reynders, Raf Simons and Linda Loppa.

34 Raf Simons for Calvin Klein 20539NYC, 'Emergency Blanket' dress, Mylar, knitted balaclava and popcorn bag, Autumn-Winter 2018-2019, MoMu, Antwerp, X180.
35 Raf Simons for Calvin Klein 20539NYC, sleeveless dress, silk chiffon and plaid with 'Log Cabin' patchwork motif, Autumn-Winter 2018-2019.
36 Raf Simons for Calvin Klein 205W39NYC, coat with fluorescent stripes, balaclava, pullover depicting Road Runner and long striped skirt, Autumn-Winter 2018-2019, MoMu, Antwerp, X178.

34

35

36

p. 218   Alana Sayn-Wittgenstein wearing Armani blouse and trousers and Maison Margiela jacket, next to the 'Poltrona CH07' chair by Hans Wegner, photographed by Steven Meisel, *Vogue Italia*, August 2013.

p. 219   Amanda Murphy in Chanel next to Gerrit Rietveld's 'Red Blue Chair', photographed by Steven Meisel, *Vogue Italia*, August 2013.

PHOTO CREDITS

Cover image: Photo Craig McDean / Art +Commerce, model Amber Valletta
p. 8-9: © Patty Carroll / Courtesy of the artist
p. 14: (1) Photo Stany Dederen / (2) Courtesy of the Smithsonian Libraries and Archives
p. 16: © Metropolitan Museum of Art, Gilman Collection, New York
p. 17: (4) © Les Arts Décoratifs / (5) © The J. Paul Getty Museum, Los Angeles / (6) © Musée d'Orsay, Dist. RMN-Grand Palais / Alexis Brandt
p. 18: Photo Stany Dederen
p. 19: (8) © Stiftung Fürst-Pückler-Museum Park und Schloss Branitz, Cottbus
p. 22: © National Trust Images / Christopher Hurst
p. 23: Photo Stany Dederen
p. 24: (12-14) Photos Stany Dederen
p. 26: (17) © Les Arts Décoratifs / (18) © iStock by Getty
p. 30: (19) Royal Museum of Fine Arts Antwerp, artinflanders.be, photo Hugo Maertens / (20) Domaine & Musée royal de Mariemont, Morlanwelz
p. 31: Photo Stany Dederen
p. 32: Photo Courtesy of the Dallas Museum of Art
p. 33: (2) Photo Stany Dederen
p. 34: (4) Photo Stany Dederen / (5) © Metropolitan Museum of Art, New York / (6) Photo Stany Dederen
p. 35: (7-8) Ville de Paris / Bibliothèque Forney
p. 36: Photo Stany Dederen
p. 37: © Musée de la Photographie Charleroi
p. 38: Photo Richard Malone
p. 39-40: Photos Catwalkpictures
p. 42: (2) Photo Stany Dederen / (3) Photo Valeria Herklotz / Artistry / (4) Photo Stany Dederen
p. 43: Photo Marina Faust
p. 44: Photo David LaChapelle
p. 45: (7-8) Photos Stany Dederen / (9) Photo Elizaveta Porodina
p. 46: Photo Morgan O'Donovan
p. 47: Photo Catwalkpictures
p. 48: Photo Willy Vanderperre / Art+Commerce, model Mica Argañaraz
p. 49: (13-15) Photos Stany Dederen
p. 50: Photo Catwalkpictures
p. 51-53: (17-18) Archives Charlotte Perriand / © Sabam Belgium 2025
p. 54: (19-20) Photos Catwalkpictures / (21) Photo Stany Dederen
p. 56-57: Photos Catwalkpictures
p. 58: Photo Elie Benistant
p. 59: Photo Thibaut Grevet
p. 61: © La Fondation L'Écuyer, Brussels / Henry van de Velde Foundation
p. 62: (1-3) © Dépôt de la Bibliothèque Royale aux AML, Brussels / Henry van de Velde Foundation
p. 64: (4) © KIK-IRPA, Brussels, photo Hervé Pigeolet / Henry van de Velde Foundation (5) © KMKG-MRAH, Brussels / Henry van de Velde Foundation (6) © Nordenfjeldske Kunstindustrimuseum, Trondheim, photo Dino Makridis / Henry van de Velde Foundation
p. 65: (7-8) © KMKG-MRAH, Brussels / Henry van de Velde Foundation (9) © Dépôt de la Bibliothèque Royale aux AML, Brussels / Henry van de Velde Foundation

p. 66-67: (10-11) © Dépôt de la Bibliothèque Royale aux AML, Brussels / Henry van de Velde Foundation
p. 68-69: (12) © Kunstmuseen Krefeld / Henry van de Velde Foundation / (13) © KMKG-MRAH, Brussels / Henry van de Velde Foundation
p. 71: (15) Royal Museum of Fine Arts Antwerp, artinflanders.be, photo Hugo Maertens / (16) Ghent Design Museum, artinflanders.be, photo Cedric Verhelst / © Henry van de Velde Foundation
p. 73: (17-19) Museum für Gestaltung, Zürich / Photo Umberto Romito & Ivan Šuta / © Henry van de Velde Foundation (20) Kunstmuseen Krefeld / © Henry van de Velde Foundation
p. 74: Kunstmuseen Krefeld
p. 76: (2) Photo Nicola Perscheid / (3-4) © Kunstmuseen Krefeld / Henry van de Velde Foundation
p. 77: © KMKG-MRAH, Brussels / Henry van de Velde Foundation
p. 80: (6) Ghent Design Museum, artinflanders.be / (7) Ghent Design Museum, artinflanders.be, photo Dries Van den Brande
p. 81: (8) Photo Umberto Romito & Ivan Šuta / (9) Kunstmuseen Krefeld / © Henry van de Velde Foundation
p. 82: © MAK – Museum of Applied Arts, Vienna
p. 83: Heidelberg University
p. 84: (3) Estate of Madame d'Ora, Museum für Kunst und Gewerbe Hamburg
p. 85: Courtesy of Galerie Yves Macaux – Private Collection
p. 86: (6) Kunstmuseen Krefeld / (7) © MAK – Museum of Applied Arts, Vienna / (8) German Textile Museum Krefeld / (9) © MAK – Museum of Applied Arts, Vienna
p. 87: © MAK – Museum of Applied Arts, Vienna
p. 88: (11) Leopold Museum, Vienna / (12) © MAK – Museum of Applied Arts, Vienna / Georg Mayer
p. 90: (13) Photo CC BY 4.0 Wien Museum, Birgit and Peter Kainz
p. 91: Estate of Madame d'Ora, Museum für Kunst und Gewerbe Hamburg
p. 92: Photo Stany Dederen
p. 93: Photo Dan Jackson / Art+Commerce, styling Clare Richardson, model Suvi Koponen
p. 94: © MAK – Museum of Applied Arts, Vienna / Georg Mayer
p. 95: (19-21) © MAK – Museum of Applied Arts, Vienna / Peter Kainz
p. 96: Leopold Museum, Vienna
p. 97: (23) © MAK – Museum of Applied Arts, Vienna / (24) © MAK – Museum of Applied Arts, Vienna / Georg Mayer
p. 98: © MAK – Museum of Applied Arts, Vienna
p. 99: © MAK – Museum of Applied Arts, Vienna / Branislav Djordjevic
p. 100: © Martin Margiela, photo Patrick Robyn
p. 102: (29) National Library of the Czech Republic / (30) © MAK – Museum of Applied Arts, Vienna / Georg Mayer
p. 104: © MAK – Museum of Applied Arts, Vienna

p. 106: (32-33) Photos Stany Dederen / (34) © MAK – Museum of Applied Arts, Vienna / Kristina Wissik
p. 108: (35) © MAK – Museum of Applied Arts, Vienna / Georg Mayer / (36) © MAK – Museum of Applied Arts, Vienna / Nathan Murrell
p. 109: (37-38) Musée de Chelles Alfred-Bonno
p. 111: © Roger-Viollet, photo Boris Lipnitzki
p. 112: © Roger-Viollet, photo Boris Lipnitzki
p. 114: Diktats Bookstore
p. 116: (4-5) © Les Arts Décoratifs
p. 119: (6) Musée départemental Albert-Kahn, Archive de la Planète, Boulogne-Billancourt / (7) Galerie Maxime Flatry, Paris
p. 120: © Victoria and Albert Museum, London / Jean Badovici
p. 121: © Les Arts Décoratifs, Paris / Jean Tholance
p. 123: Palais Galliera, Musée de la Mode de la Ville de Paris
p. 124: © Studio Lipnitzki / Roger-Viollet
p. 126: (13) CC0 Paris Musées / Palais Galliera, Musée de la Mode de la Ville de Paris / (14) © Les Arts Décoratifs / Jean-Marie Del Moral
p. 127: (15) LANVIN Heritage, Paris / (16) © Les Arts Décoratifs/Philippe Chancel
p. 129: © The estate of Edward Steichen / Sabam Belgium, 2019
p. 130-131: © LANVIN Heritage, Paris
p. 133: Photo Horst P. Horst, *Vogue* © Condé Nast
p. 134-135: © CHANEL / Photo François Halard
p. 145: Österreichische Nationalbibliothek, Bildarchiv Austria, Vienna, Pf 830: D (1)
p. 146: © The ALBERTINA Museum, Vienna
p. 147: Armchair: Courtesy Galerie Yves Macaux – Private collection / Villa Müller: © The ALBERTINA Museum, Vienna
p. 149-152: Von Parish Kostümbibliothek, Munich
p. 154: (4) © Sabam Belgium 2025 / (5) Digital image © The Museum of Modern Art, New York / Scala Florence
p. 155: Silver gelatin print, 6 11 / 16 x 9', Mies van der Rohe Archive, gift of the architect. Digital image Mies van der Rohe, gift of the architect / MoMA / Scala
p. 156-157: © Architecture, Design & Engineering Drawings Collection, Prints & Photographs Division, Library of Congress, ADE - UNIT 2932, no. 1 (B size)
p. 159: (8-9) © Sabam Belgium 2025
p. 160: (10) Silver gelatin print, 8 x 10', Mies van der Rohe Archive, gift of the architect. Digital image The Museum of Modern Art, New York / Scala, Florence / © Sabam Belgium 2025 (11) © Sabam Belgium 2025 (11) © Stiftung Bauhaus Dessau (I 7653 F) / Sabam Belgium 2025
p. 161: © Sabam Belgium 2025
p. 162: Interiors Akanthos, Antwerp
p. 163: © Vitra Design Museum, Weil am Rhein, photo Jürgen Hans / © Sabam Belgium 2025
p. 167: Silver gelatin print, 7 ¼ x 9 3 / 8', Mies van der Rohe Archive, gift of the architect. Digital image The Museum of Modern Art, New York / Scala, Florence / © Sabam Belgium 2025

p. 168-169: Photo © Craig McDean / Art+Commerce, models Frida Gustavsson, Aymeline Valade, Caroline Trentini, Jourdan Dunn
p. 171: Photo Craig McDean / Art+Commerce, model Rachel Weisz
p. 172: Dominique Lelys
p. 175: © Fondation Le Corbusier
p. 177: © NPL – DeA Picture Library / G. Nimatallah / Bridgeman Images
p. 178: © RMN – Gestion droit d'auteur Sam Lévin Localisation : Charenton-le-Pont, Médiathèque du Patrimoine et de la Photographie © Ministère de la Culture – Médiathèque du patrimoine et de la photographie, Dist. GrandPalaisRmn / Sam Lévin
p. 179: Dominique Lelys
p. 180-181: Fondation Le Corbusier, Paris, © F.L.C. / Sabam Belgium 2025
p. 183: Irving Penn © Condé Nast
p. 186-187: (2-4) Fondation Le Corbusier, Paris / (2) © F.L.C. / Sabam Belgium 2025 / (3) Flemish Community – Flanders Architecture Institute, Georges Baines Archive, Antwerp / (4) © F.L.C. / Sabam Belgium 2025
p. 191: Photo Stany Dederen
p. 192: © Ann Demeulemeester – Serax / Photo Marc Wouters
p. 193: Photo Stany Dederen
p. 198: Photo Marina Faust
p. 199: © Maison Martin Margiela
p. 201: Photos Stany Dederen
p. 202: Photo Ronald Stoops
p. 203: Photo Stany Dederen
p. 204: Photo Art Gray
p. 205: Photo Stany Dederen
p. 208-209: © Raf Simons
p. 210-211: Photo Delfino Sisto Legnani, DSL Studio
p. 212-213: Photo Willy Vanderperre / Art+Commerce, models Ariel Murtagh, Lulu Tenney, Leila Goldkuhl, Sara Grace Wallerstedt
p. 214: Karen Radkai, *Vogue* © Condé Nast
p. 217: (34-36): Photos Stany Dederen / (36) Photo Catwalkpictures
p. 218: Photo Steven Meisel, model Alana Sayn-Wittgenstein
p. 219: Photo Steven Meisel, model Amanda Murphy

This book is published in conjunction with the exhibition *Fashion & Interiors. A Gendered Affair* on view at MoMu—Fashion Museum Antwerp from 29 March to 3 August 2025.

CURATOR
Romy Cockx

EXHIBITION DESIGN
Altu

GRAPHIC DESIGN
Jelle Jespers (campaign image)
Victor Robyn (gallery texts)

PRODUCTION COMPANY
Solution

LIGHT
Licht bvba

3D ANIMATION
d_archive

VIDEO MONTAGE
Els Voorspoels

VIDEO
Vidi-Square

MOMU—FASHION MUSEUM ANTWERP

DIRECTOR
Kaat Debo

BUSINESS MANAGEMENT
Sara Joukes

CURATORS
Romy Cockx
Elisa De Wyngaert

ASSISTANT CURATOR
Juliette de Waal

PRODUCTION MANAGEMENT
Marie Vandecasteele

ASSISTANT PRODUCTION
Kris Robbe

CONSERVATOR
Wim Mertens

COLLECTION MANAGEMENT
Frédéric Boutié
Ellen Machiels
Pieter Pauwels
Wouter Pauwels
Belgiz Polat
Isabel Suengue
Kim Verkens
Danicia van Glanen-Weijgel

LIBRARY & DRIES VAN NOTEN STUDY CENTRE
Birgit Ansoms
Hadewijch Bal
Ester Claes
Isabel Davis
Marguerite De Coster
Tobias Hendrickx
Dieter Suls
Michelle Suykerbuyk
Stijn Van den Bulck
Eva Van den Ende
Ykje Wildenborg

PRESS & COMMUNICATIONS
Michael Bex
David Flamée
Lies Verboven

EDUCATION & EVENTS
Iris Adriaenssens
Leen Borgmans
Karl Kana
Shanti Ofori
Klaartje Patteet

PARTICIPATION
Alex Akuete
Jana Tricot

ADMINISTRATION
Diane Van Osta

MERCHANDISING MANAGER
Annik Pirotte

HOSPITALITY MANAGER
An Teyssen

WELCOME DESK
Lina Borgonjon
Maaike Delsaerdt
Kristel Van den Wyngaert

FACILITY MANAGEMENT
Justin Vanneste

MAINTENANCE
Maria Sebastiao Viegas

SECURITY
Internal security service of
AG Culturele Instellingen Antwerpen

LENDERS
20Age Archive
Akanthos, Antwerp
Ann Demeulemeester
bel etage Gallery, Vienna
BOTTER
Charliermuseum, Sint-Joost-ten-Node
Craig Green
Dallas Museum of Art
Design Museum Ghent
Diktats Bookstore, Lens
Dirk Van Saene
Dominique Lelys
Flanders Architecture Institute, Antwerp
Fondation Azzedine Alaïa, Paris
Fondation Le Corbusier, Paris
Galerie Maxime Flatry, Paris
Galerie Yves Macaux – private collection, Brussels
German Textile Museum Krefeld
HoGent
Hussein Chalayan
Isolde Pringiers
J. & L. Lobmeyr, Vienna
KBR, Royal Library of Belgium, Brussels
Kunstmuseen Krefeld
LANVIN Heritage, Paris
Leopold Museum, Vienna
Maison Margiela
MAK – Museum of Applied Arts, Vienna
Marcus Tomlinson
Marine Serre
Martin Margiela
Max Reynders
Mudam Luxembourg – Musée d'Art Moderne Grand-Duc Jean
Musée de Chelles Alfred-Bonno
Musée royal de Mariemont, Morlanwelz
Museum Boijmans Van Beuningen, Rotterdam
Museum für Gestaltung Zürich
Patty Carroll
Raf Simons Collection
Richard Malone
Royal Museum of Fine Arts Antwerp
Serax, Kontich
The Mark Wallis Collection
Vitra Design Museum, Weil am Rhein
Von Parish Kostümbibliothek, Munich
Wien Museum, Vienna
And all private lenders

WITH SPECIAL THANKS TO
Noémie Brakema
Yaël Coopman
Ann Demeulemeester & Patrick Robyn
Bianca Luzi
Martin Margiela
Alessandro Michele
Bob Verhelst
Priska Schmückle von Minckwitz
Henry van de Velde Family Foundation
Willy Vanderperre

PUBLICATION

COMPOSITION AND EDITING
Romy Cockx

AUTHORS
Werner Adriaenssens
Jess Berry
Romy Cockx
Dries Debackere
Ian Erickson
Magdalena Holzhey
Wim Mertens
Robin Schuldenfrei
Lara Steinhäußer

GRAPHIC DESIGN
Jelle Jespers

IMAGE RESEARCH AND COPYRIGHT
Birgit Ansoms
Romy Cockx
Marguerite De Coster
Juliette de Waal

PROJECT MANAGEMENT
Stephanie Van den bosch

TRANSLATION
Alison Mouthaan

EDITING
Xavier De Jonge

PHOTOGRAVURE
Johan Bursens

PRINTING & BINDING
Printer Trento, Italy

PUBLISHER
Gautier Platteau

ISBN 978 94 6494 193 7
D/2025/11922/19
NUR 452

© Hannibal Books and
MoMu—Fashion Museum Antwerp, 2025
www.hannibalbooks.be
www.momu.be

COVER
Amber Valletta wearing a suit,
photographed by Craig McDean for
Interview Magazine, July 2014
Photo: Craig McDean/Art+Commerce
Model: Amber Valletta

All rights reserved. No part of this publication may be reproduced or transmitted in any form or by any means, electronic or mechanical, including photocopy, recording or any other information storage and retrieval system, without prior permission in writing from the publisher.

Every effort has been made to trace copyright holders for all texts, photographs and reproductions. If, however, you feel that you have inadvertently been overlooked, please contact the museum.